For Unto Us a Child Is Born

Grace and Glory from Handel's *Messiah*

By

David B. Smith

Waldo Publishing
San Bernardino, California

AUTHOR WEB PAGE

www.davidbsmithbooks.com

Books by David B. Smith

Aiming For the Pin
Bats, Balls & Altar Calls
Daniel Diaries
Essential Unity 101 (Essays in Ephesians)
Finding Waldo
Grace Tough As Nails
Heaven
More Than Amazing Grace
Moving Through the Valley of Doubt
Music Wars
Nowhere Man
Overcoming the Barriers of Anger
Pictures of Jesus in the Stories He Told
Rock-Solid Living in a Run-Amok World
Salvation on the Summit
Spirit's Double
Time of Terror, Time of Healing
Watching the War
Your Biggest Decision Ever

RACHEL MARIE SERIES

#1 Love in a Distant Land
#2 And a Happy New You
#3 All the Winning Numbers
#4 Bump, Set, Love
#5 Resurrected Love

BUCKY STONE ADVENTURES

#1 Making Waves at Hampton Beach High
#2 Showdown at Home Plate
#3 Outcast on the Court
#4 Bucky's Big Break
#5 Bad News in Bangkok
#6 Bucky's Close Shave
#7 Bucky Gets Busted
#8 Summer Camp Scars
#9 Fire in Paradise
#10 The Final Game

Contents

For Unto Us a Child Is Born

Comfort ye, comfort ye, my people, saith your God; speak ye comfortably to Jerusalem; and cry unto her, that her warfare is accomplished, that her iniquity is pardoned. The voice of him that crieth in the wilderness, Prepare ye the way of the Lord, make straight in the desert a highway for our God. Isaiah 40:1-3

1

Comfort Ye My People

Anybody who teaches math for a living will, sooner or later, do a bit of hand-holding and comforting. Especially when the end of the semester approaches, trials pile up and hard stories become part of my daily menu.

In just *one day* this past week, I had to almost shed my title of Professor Smith and once again don my clerical collar. Students didn't exactly call me Pastor Dave, but I definitely felt like I was back in the (Protestant) confessional.

Nancy (all names changed) sat down for an algebra test . . . and simply froze up. She's a struggling single mom with a beautiful but dependent three-year-old daughter. Rent takes most of her public-assistance paycheck. Math ideas, when they penetrate her mind at all, are hazy and temporary visitors. And as she stared at the twenty-two factoring problems on those white sheets of paper, they simply oozed into an unintelligible and hostile collection of numerical soldiers amassed against her.

She sat at her desk, feebly scribbling a few random numbers, all of them miles off track. Half an hour in, she penned a despairing note, thrust the nearly untouched paper in front of me, and bolted from the room. I could hear her sobbing out in the hallway. Later, she went online, dropped the class, and postponed her fragile dreams for another six months.

• • • • •

Jasmine shares a similar dis-affinity for mathematics, but gives every homework assignment a herculean effort; her homework assignments are often six pages long, written in a precise but clumsy handwriting. Quizzes generally have a big question mark covering half her work and a penciled plea: "Don't Understand!!!" She sat down in my office yesterday, her eyes reddened. "What's wrong?" I asked.

Oh, nothing really. Except that she is hanging on to her C by a thread. Her husband, a sweet and simple man, just had yet another booze relapse. With rent overdue, she was about to be evicted. Some friends had offered to share a roof over her head for a temporary fortnight, but without another sympathetic person's donation of money for storage, she didn't even have a place to put her meager belongings.

• • • • •

Benjamin, a hard-working man straight from the ghetto's mean streets, exhibits a flair for math . . . when he makes it to class. About every third day, something jumps up and bites his ambitions and he drags himself in with a profuse apology. "I don't blame you," I keep telling him. "But man, you're going to have to get a lot luckier–in terms of attendance–if you want to pass this class."

"I know, professor. I know. I know." He shakes his slick-shaved head in abject repentance. "I'll be here. Yes sir." But now he's missed five sessions in a row, probably a fatal blow to his dreams. How come?

Someone who knows him gives a frustrated shrug. “He got locked up, Mr. Smith. Don’t know for what. But he’s in county jail. Said he hoped he could get out and still come take the final.”

• • • • •

Then I got a test put in my faculty box from Disabled Programs and Services. Chanelle is a pretty but very timid girl, barely out of high school and prone to tears and weeklong absences. I scanned the test, which had the aforementioned twenty-two problems on it. Not a single one was done right. Instead of FOILing trinomials, she had scrawled a desperate and meaningless bunch of prime factors that didn’t add up to anything. Gulping, I gave her a few sympathy points for her efforts and slipped her the returned exam with a sympathetic 35% in the upper-right corner.

Her eyes swam with tears and I drew her to one side. “What happened? I know that you know this stuff better than this.”

Between sniffles she poured out her graphic tale of self-inflicted woe. Parents had kicked her out for this or that. So she moved in with some nameless boyfriend that she “kind of liked.” He soon had his way with her, and she fears that in a night of unlit groping, he hadn’t bothered with a condom. Now she was late, maybe pregnant, with a confusing world crashing down all around her.

All at once, I find new and stirring meaning to these four words from Isaiah: *Comfort ye My people.*

• • • • •

Every year at Christmastime, my wife Lisa and I drive to downtown Los Angeles for a very special event. Each December, thousands of music lovers gather together for an elegant and memorable group experience: The Sing-Along Messiah.

For years it was held annually at the Dorothy Chandler Pavilion. Here in the 21st century, it’s moved over to the elegant Walt Disney Hall . . . but we’ve now made it a practice to sing the *Messiah* at Lake Avenue Congregational Church in Pasadena. It’s beautifully decorated for the

Christmas season, and there's an extra-special Christian atmosphere which is truly a blessing. My own faith community at Loma Linda University Church does *Messiah* highlights the weekend before Christmas, and we make sure we're always sitting right up close.

There's something life-transforming about this particular oratorio– usually described as the world's favorite. In fact, from the album notes in one of the CD versions I own, I find this comment: "It has been performed more steadily in all the world than any other choral work in existence. Thousands of musicians and amateurs all over the world unite in churches, concert halls, and broadcasting stations to celebrate the grandiose, the Unique 'Messiah.'"

And participants sense some of that each Christmas. There's the orchestra and the four soloists and all the tuxedos and glittery evening gowns. And then there are the common folks like us, men and women and teenagers and kids with worn-out copies of the old Schirmer's Edition, trying to find our parts and sing along the best we can. More than once, though, I have to stop and just let the goosebumps settle back down or wipe a tear away. To sing the "Hallelujah Chorus" with over two thousand other people is an experience that's very close to heaven.

You really have to praise God that for twenty-four days, from August 22 until September 14 in the year 1741, George Frederick Handel sat at his writing table, feverishly putting down the notes that make up the *Messiah.* In just over three weeks, from somewhere inside that gifted mind, came pouring out 252 pages of masterpiece work.

I try to envision that grand composer, fifty-six years old at the time, working day and night, almost desperate to pour out this work while it was in him. Often he would ignore the meals his servants brought to him; he was just too busy, too driven.

But perhaps this oratorio, this greatest of all musical achievements, actually came from a higher source. And Handel himself realized it. Maybe during those twenty-four days, he was especially linked up with the musical courts of Paradise, and he determined to bring this great work to a sin-stained world while the Spirit was moving upon him. In fact, at one point he made this confession: "I think I did see all Heaven before me, and the great God Himself."

This isn't at all to diminish what Handel the *man* accomplished; those three-and-a-half weeks of superhuman achievement still live today as we play and sing these great choruses!

There are fifty-three songs in the *Messiah*, so it's interesting that George Frederick Handel chose "Comfort Ye My People" to be the very first words sung in his oratorio, right after the opening overture by the orchestra. It speaks volumes that the Christmas message–in fact, all that the Bible tells us about a Messiah–begins with comfort. And this is God talking! *Comfort ye My people, saith your God.*

The Bible actually begins, *Comfort ye, comfort ye, My people.* "Repeated for emphasis," note the text scholars. I think of my four students, their dreams shredded, their souls overwhelmed by the travails of life. And just as I almost have to offer a hug and soothe them with: "Hey, it's okay. *It's okay.* We'll find a way to fix this," God Himself offers a double dose of comfort to His broken-down children.

Often at Christmastime, as we look back on the tumult of the concluding year, we decide we could use some comforting! Certainly the people of God, the Body of Christ, could benefit from some encouraging . . . but how about you, right now, today? And the next time you thumb through your iPod and listen to this haunting tenor solo, I hope you can feel the personal signature of God in this directive. "Comfort ye My people"–and He does indeed have you in mind.

It's a moving spiritual experience to look up in your Bible to study the original passages Handel and librettist Charles Jennens selected. Not one word of this great oratorio came just from a composer's own imagination–and that's not to take away from Handel's 24-day achievement. But this is the Word of God speaking to us in these arias and recitatives. And the very first song comes from Isaiah chapter 40.

If you've ever read through the entire book of Isaiah, you know that for quite a long summer spell, there's not much comfort there. Chapters one through 35 are rather blistering, filled with denunciations and an excoriating list of Israel's sins. And also a list of the judgments they can expect from heaven in response to those sins.

The Lord will cause men to hear His majestic voice and will make them see His arm coming down with raging anger and consuming fire, with cloudburst, thunderstorm and hail (30:30). Cheery things like that. After reading a half hour or so of early Isaiah, flunking a college algebra test feels like nothing.

And there's much more along that vein. Then chapters 36-39 are a second mini-section, so to speak, a narrative about King Hezekiah and his enemy Sennacherib. And there's at least a brief respite from the gloom and doom so far.

But then in chapter 40, it's as though someone abruptly opened up a massive door and let the December sunlight in. Because all at once, this stern-faced prophet of doom begins to write about the coming Messiah. The very first words of chapter 40 are these: *Comfort ye, comfort ye My people, saith your God.* And from here to the end, in chapter 66, Isaiah writes so much about the hope Israel has because of the promised Redeemer that he's sometimes known as the "gospel prophet."

In his great commentary, titled simply *Messiah,* professor of religion Roger Bullard writes: "Silence follows the closing chord of the overture. The music begins again, softly. It broods and ripples, like the primeval waters of chaos over which the Spirit of God hovers at the beginning of creation, just before God spoke light into existence. The darkness of exile is profound, but there is hope alive within it. The obscurity is pierced by the tenor's first note, like the first ray of light illuminating the primordial dark. His rising line is the breaking dawn of a new day for God's people, falling back into serene assurance: 'Comfort ye, My people.'"[1]

If you read through chapter 40, or just hum your way through this tenor solo, you find this intriguing line after the "Comfort ye my people": *And cry unto her [Israel] that her warfare is accomplished, that her iniquity is pardoned.*

The past 39 chapters has been a messy list of sins or iniquities. Like a responsible father sometimes has to do, God has sent word through His prophet about the transgressions of His people. "You've done this wrong, and that wrong, and the other two hundred things wrong too," He warns. However, here in chapter 40, verse two, comes the encouraging follow-up: "But your iniquity is pardoned."

Isn't that tremendous good news? And it doesn't just apply to Israel, but to you and me during this Christmas season. Our iniquity is pardoned too, right now.

I once misbehaved so spectacularly that I was kicked out of college. It was a tough and shaming moment for me. But what a relief to get a letter from home with this quiet and generous assurance: "We forgive you." My parents weren't angry with me; there was no condemnation. My iniquity had been pardoned.

What does it mean when it says: "Her warfare is accomplished"? The Adventist Bible commentary says this: "The warfare referred to includes the military invasions of Isaiah's own time"–and there were plenty of those, as you can read–"the conquests of Babylon under Nebuchadnezzar more than a century later, and, figuratively, the broader warfare of the church against the powers of darkness in all ages."[2]

Isaiah was written a full century before the Babylonian captivity. And yet this prophetic message of encouragement comes to Israel even before that episode begins. "Your warfare is accomplished"–future tense. The NIV renders it this way: "Your hard service has been completed." And then, according to these Bible commentators, this promise even reaches down to today, to the challenges the church faces here at the dawn of the 21st century. But God gives us this comforting promise ahead of time:

"Your warfare is accomplished. My victories on your behalf are a 'done deal.'"

Again, this music and these Scripture passages are most effective when we turn them inward and apply their power to our own experience. MY iniquities have been pardoned; all the warfare within, my inner demons, my personal struggles with sin . . . God promises me comfort by saying that He's going to accomplish victory in my life. And in your life too.

Surely even Handel had to be moved to select Isaiah 40:1 as his opening solo by personal experience. At the height of his musical career, we read, he was under constant attack from other people. Other musicians, particularly, who resented this talented upstart. You remember the Oscar-winning Amadeus film story, where the envy of Saliere was bitter, almost consuming. Well, Handel felt that as well. Two English essayists, Addison and Steele, ripped away at this new composer almost from the moment he arrived in London. Their own unsuccessful attempts in the field of opera, and the resulting financial losses, drove them to jealousy, resentment, almost a blind hatred, for Handel.

But then there was this promise, meant for Handel too. "Comfort ye My people. . . . Your warfare is accomplished. There will be peace again."

Before you turn on your stereo and hear these lofty notes, please note one vital thing. There's no "comfort" unless there's a Messiah. The writings of Isaiah provide comfort, and he's known as the "gospel prophet" only because Song #2 is followed by fifty-one more songs that give us the Christ Child, the Redeemer of this world and the Savior of us all.

Every valley shall be exalted, and every mountain and hill made low; the crooked straight, and the rough places plain. Isaiah 40:4

2

Every Valley Shall Be Exalted

It was a min-scandal in 2012 when Secret Service agents traveled to Cartagena for the express purpose of preparing the way for a presidential visit. But, in addition to securing hotel rooms, and interviewing kitchen staff, and taping down manhole covers on streets that would be traveled by the Obama motorcade, a number of agents managed to spend money on exotic Colombian cocktails and paid female escorts. They were expected to be diligent in creating a safe and productive work environment for their chief executive, and they had been guilty of divided loyalties.

If any of you were raised, as I was, watching missionary reports in church, I'm sure you recall many times seeing the classic scene: the jungle landing of the missionary airplane. That tiny, one-propeller, two-seater would come gliding in over the tops of the Amazon trees. And then, with a final tremor of the wings, it would bounce down onto a dirt runway. I knew a missionary named Dick Hall who lived that very kind of colorful existence!

Maybe we've been tempted in recent years, with all the advances around the globe, to think that the missionary pilot is a relic from the past. But a few years ago, when I was preparing some Christian radio programs on this same topic, I happened to notice in an issue of *Christianity Today* a story from the wonderful organization, World Gospel Mission. John and Masako Trosen, young missionaries with their two young children, Isaiah, age three, and Sophia, just eight months old, were lost when their Cessna went down in the jungles around the Yapacani River in Bolivia. Brand new missionaries, but now tragically presumed dead.

In the same issue–with a bit of ironic timing–was a full-page advertisement for another tremendous organization, Moody Aviation, part of the Moody Bible Institute. And right there is a picture of a little airplane coming in for a landing on a dirt-strip runway.

But what in the world is the connection between these primitive airstrips and the music of Handel's *Messiah*?

It's interesting that Isaiah chapter 40 is the source material for five of Handel's songs in the *Messiah*. Consider his opening statement, and let's stay with the familiar King James, just as Handel did, of course.

Comfort ye, comfort ye my people, saith your God. Speak ye comfortably to Jerusalem, and cry unto her, that her warfare is accomplished, that her iniquity is pardoned. . . . The voice of him that crieth in the wilderness, Prepare ye the way of the Lord, make straight in the desert a highway for our God. Every valley shall be exalted, and every mountain and hill shall be made low: and the crooked shall be made straight, and the rough places plain: And the glory of the Lord shall be revealed, and all flesh shall see it together: for the mouth of the Lord hath spoken it.

Well, that's three songs right there. Again, after 39 chapters of chastisement and condemnation, Isaiah suddenly brings hope and encouragement. He comforts the nation with the promise that warfare is over.

Israel had endured endless conflict with the Assyrians; and looking to the future, their problems with Babylon were about a hundred years off. Really, all of us in the Christian church today can embrace this Bible prophecy as referring to the warfare, the battles, against Satan that have been and are and will be. But here we're all promised comfort. We're promised pardon for our iniquities too.

And then these words: "The voice of him that crieth in the wilderness." Which brings to mind an image of John the Baptist as he cries out: "Prepare the way! The Lord is coming!" This leads us to the beautiful metaphor where a great road is prepared to welcome the King. The hills are leveled for Him; the valleys and dips in the road are filled in. Crooked places in the path are made straight, the rough spots are repaved and smoothed out–because this wonderful King is arriving and He deserves a wonderful welcome. He deserves the best.

I still recall an event going back to around 1959. I was a four-year-old missionary kid living in Chiang Mai, a city in northern Thailand. But the word went out that beloved King Bhumibol was coming to our city. For weeks, a great cleanup effort went on. The streets were tidied up; walls were painted. Long-standing piles of trash were finally attended to. Even stray dogs were corralled and tied up. School kids wore their best blue-and-white uniforms; their faces were powdered and clean. Each one held a tiny Thai flag to wave as the motorcade rolled past. It was wonderful, and even an American kid like me got into the spirit of the thing. The king was coming and all good things needed to be made ready.

So that brings to our minds the image of that dirt runway. You see, the missionary plane couldn't get in there unless people who *wanted* the missionary there would prepare the way and level the road. This kind visitor is bringing medicine to heal the wounds. Schoolbooks to teach the unschooled. Music to cheer their hearts. Stories and Bible teachings to point them to a new life. Of course, they wanted these blessings, these gifts, but they couldn't receive them unless they made a way–an airplane runway. And I've actually seen footage of eager men and women out there with their crude tools, hacking away at the trees and the shrubs, and then carefully smoothing out the nicest landing strip they could fashion.

We might even wonder if George Frederick Handel himself, as he envisioned the winding, crooked cobblestone streets of Dublin, Ireland where the *Messiah* debuted on April 13, 1742, had that same image in his mind. "Straighten out that twisting, turning road! The Messiah is about to arrive!"

Musicologists have noted that Handel almost subliminally illustrates the Bible lyrics as he composes. When the tenor sings, "Every valley shall be exalted," the notes soar from low to high. When he gets to the part: "The crooked plain," the melody line wobbles, then holds on a long, smooth note . . . making us think of a broad, beautiful eight-lane interstate freeway or German autobahn. Bullard actually counts, and smilingly reminds us that Handel uses four notes for "crooked" and just one for "straight"![1]

Well, what can this mean for us as we do our Christmas shopping? Does Jesus want a smooth highway made of asphalt or even a yellow brick road? Of course not. When He first came to our world two thousand Christmases ago, there was no parade down Main Street; He came to where there were bumpy dirt roads and barns and mangers. No, the prophet Isaiah and John the Baptist are talking about people who prepare a way for Christ in their *hearts*. They smooth out a path for Him to enter into their lives. If there are mountains in the way–pride, revenge, a love of the world–they get out a shovel and level those mountains. If there are valleys of discouragement or sin, they fill them in. Crooked places in the road where they lurch off to this or that new fad or distraction? They straighten out the highway. If there are deserts of spiritual dryness, the sterility of an uncaring heart, they turn on the sprinklers. They're preparing the way for the King!

It is wonderfully true that Jesus will enter our lives without preconditions. *Here I am!* He announces. *I stand at the door and knock. If anyone hears My voice and opens the door, I will come in and eat with him, and he with Me* (Rev. 3:20). But it's also true that for there to be an abiding and sustained relationship with the King of our universe, we must prepare a hospitable environment. I have had to face my own conflicting desires at times and grudgingly acknowledged that, in order to really be in close communion with Jesus, a pet grievance or nurtured grudge would have to be shoveled over to the curb.

And the even better news is this. Jesus our soon-arriving King is so kind that He actually steps in and helps us prepare that runway FOR HIM! He enters in and helps us smooth out the way. *Trust in the Lord with all your heart and lean not on your own understanding; in all your ways acknowledge Him, and HE will make your paths straight* (Prov. 3:5, 6).

And here's Isaiah 26:7: *The path of the righteous is level; O upright One,* You *make the way of the righteous smooth.*

Please excuse me for a moment, because I think I hear the Savior knocking on my door right now. And it looks like He's got two shovels.

And the glory of the Lord shall be revealed, and all flesh shall see it together; for the mouth of the Lord hath spoken it. Isaiah 40:5

3

And the Glory of the Lord

It was a cold night out in the sparse foliage of the desert and the sheep pressed together, desperate for a bit of warmth. Jacob and his brother dozed intermittently underneath the starry sky, inky with desolate disfavor. Far in the distance, the fading lamps of Jerusalem slowly blinked out as midnight crept over the nation.

The two shepherds talked in low, weary tones, hoping for a night without predators or marauding men. It was a difficult life, endless and with dwindling hopes. Rome was a headstrong, pervasive presence, with soldiers and regulations and oppressive taxation. For years, even decades, simple men like Jacob and Bethuel had sat in synagogue and heard stories of Messiah. A deliverer who would come in trumpet-bathed glory. A rescuing King whose arrival would restore their manhood and their hopes and their national pride.

But the years passed and the rule of Rome tightened around their souls.

Jacob heaved a sigh, his unexpressed dreams locked within. What was the use of going over the same failed agenda over and over again? God had left them alone; heaven was a distant and abandoned promise. The splendor of a rebuilt and resplendent Israel had died.

All at once, a strange and otherworldly glow began to spread across the midnight sky with a penetrating power beyond their ability to comprehend.

• • • • •

As Lisa and I sit with the gathered congregation at the Lake Avenue Congregational Church, all the would-be singers, it's interesting to notice how eager everyone is for the first chorus–the first opportunity when *we* will join in. Yes, the beginning "Overture" by the orchestra is beautiful. And the first two solos by the tenor, "Comfort Ye My People" and "Every Valley Shall Be Exalted," are both breathtaking, not only in their musical complexity, but in the way the melody lines enhance the biblical message. But you can tell that everyone is eager to get to the song, "And the Glory of the Lord." This is our moment–and we certainly enjoy it!

I'm almost embarrassed by the reality that as the tenor soloist concludes with ". . . And the rough places plain," we commoners begin to fidget in our seats. There's an audible rustling of pages as hundreds of singers make sure we're on page sixteen and that all the baritones are lined up to enter on measure 14. There's a pleasant and well-intentioned hum of anticipation, almost to the point where red-faced giggles break out.

It's incredible how much of Handel's *Messiah* does come from the Old Testament. Being an oratorio about Jesus Christ, you might expect that most of this great work would come right out of Matthew, Mark, Luke, and John. But no, we're still right here in Isaiah 40. *And the glory of the Lord shall be revealed, and all flesh shall see it together; for the mouth of the Lord hath spoken it.*

And surely this December, as it happens every Christmas season, we see the fulfillment of Isaiah 40:5. "The glory of the Lord shall be revealed," God promises. "You will see My work in the world in an unforgettable way."

This is a very common and beautiful theme throughout the Bible, where, even when we don't deserve it, the Lord reveals His glory. A little Bible footnote sends us from Isaiah 40 back to Exodus chapter 16, where the children of Israel have been complaining about the food.

And God, without any anger or resentment, says to Moses: *"In the morning you will see the glory of the Lord."*

Sure enough, the next morning when the children of Israel go outside their tents and look around, there's manna covering the ground. God has provided! God has worked a miracle. You can't miss it; you can't help but be aware of it. Every parent, every child, every relative and visitor dines on that miracle food three times a day, seven days a week. They all know. So the promise: "All flesh shall see it together"–that part is revealed as well.

Over and over, we find this theme. "The glory of the Lord will be revealed." Answered prayers. People healed. Miracles happening. Rebellious hearts melted. Even today, people testify how the glory of God has been revealed in some unique new way. Over and over and over again, Isaiah 40:5 comes true once more.

I've gone back to my beloved homeland of Thailand, where I grew up as a boy. For seventeen years my dad walked on a lot of dirt roads and maneuvered through Bangkok traffic. He gave Bible studies to people who had the barest understanding of the Christ child. And then there were baptisms, glorious moments where Thai teenagers, some rescued from lives of crime or prostitution, went into the water and received a new life. The guarantee of eternal life in heaven. And the glory of the Lord was revealed.

Couples about to file for divorce have an encounter with the Man from Galilee, and He empowers them to work things out and find a restored, Edenic relationship. The glory of the Lord is revealed.

Churches spring up and often the power of heaven seems to invade the entire community. People are gripped with the power of the gospel; the church swells in a magnificent way. And the glory of the Lord is revealed to us all.

But the greatest revelation of God, the greatest display of His glory, has got to be the Christmas story. The birth of Jesus Christ. "And the glory of the Lord was revealed." Angel choirs sang. The star led the Wise Men to the side of the manger where they could worship. And then thirty-three years later, as Jesus was lifted up on the cross, the whole world saw it happen. *And all flesh shall see it together,* Isaiah had predicted so many centuries earlier. And even the Messiah Himself said to His followers in John 12:32: *"But I, when I am lifted up from the earth, will draw all men to Myself."*

As you listen to this first great chorus, it's an incredible experience to sing along. But even more, let these great words and majestic notes create in your heart a response of gratitude for the Messiah, for the *revealed* glory of the Lord that all of us can see and experience together. The greatness of the song is the slightest hint of the glory yet to come.

And He shall purity the sons of Levi, that they may offer unto the Lord an offering in righteousness. Malachi 3:3

4

And He Shall Purify

I have two daughters I'm hugely proud of, not only for the four gorgeous grandchildren they have presented to me. But also because both of them triumphed in tough, knuckle-scraping ordeals that made them better people.

Karli, a young and inexperienced mother, persevered through a tough pregnancy and completed a Ph.D. in mathematics. There were impossible classes to take, a dissertation to write on the trace forms of abelian functions. Every time we're together, I cheerfully pretend to know what she's talking about.

Kami, after several years as a classroom teacher, decided to also improve her lot by getting a state certification in math. She went to extra classes, drove endless hours to weekend seminars, did homework till midnight. Occasionally she would call me on the phone, and I blushed when there were problems I couldn't do. She sat down for the test, turned hot and cold and prickly and apprehensive at how hard the problems were

. . . and then passed with flying colors.

See why I'm proud?

But the fact is that this process of grinding out a new skill, a better *you* . . . can hurt! It can peel away our false bravados, our slender veneer of self-confidence. We have to sacrifice pet habits and petty pleasures if we really want to be all that God wants us to be.

• • • • •

It was on a Tuesday evening, April 13, in 1742, in Dublin, Ireland, when the public first heard what we still treasure here in the 21st century. Seven months after his frantic, 24-day marathon of composing, George Frederick Handel first presented his *Messiah.*

Of course, there were newspaper critics back in those days just like we have now. And in Faulkner's Journal, published in Dublin just four days later, we find that Mr. Handel's work received very positive marks. Here's the word-for-word critique, and you can almost smell the white powder on the wigs:

"On Tuesday last, Mr. Handel's Sacred Grand Oratorio, the MESSIAH, was performed in the New Music Hall in Fishamblestreet; the best Judges allowed it to be the most finished piece of music. Words are wanting to express the exquisite Delight it afforded to the admiring crowded Audience. The Sublime, the Grand, and the Tender, adapted to the most elevated, majestic and moving Words, conspired to transport and charm the ravished Heart and Ear."

Well, that sounds like "two thumbs up," doesn't it? And let's meet for a Starbuck's after the concert, right there in Fishamblestreet. (Love that name!)

This first performance was a charity concert for the benefit of "the Prisoners in several Gaols"–that's *jails*, of course–"and for the support of Mercer's Hospital in Stephen Street, and of the Charitable Infirmary on the Inn's Quay." And here's another bit of trivia you might want to file away in your mind. The contralto part in that first performance was sung by a Mrs. Susannah Cibber. More about her in a few moments.

You know, when we celebrate all that Handel's *Messiah* stands for during the holiday season, we especially focus on Jesus Christ our Redeemer, as the Holy Child in the manger, the Lamb of God who came to take away our sins. Jesus standing in our place–that's what the *Messiah* is all about. So much of this great music deals with the theme of Christ's suffering; we think immediately of songs like "Surely He Hath Borne Our Griefs." And then "All We Like Sheep Have Gone Astray" . . . with its hauntingly beautiful closing line: "And the Lord hath laid on HIM the iniquity of us all."

And yet, here is a song with a much different emphasis. One of my favorite choruses is this one, Number Seven, entitled "And He Shall Purify," taken from Malachi 3:3. The entire verse reads this way:

And He shall sit as a refiner and purifier of silver: and he shall purify the sons of Levi, and purge them as gold and silver, that they may offer unto the Lord an offering in righteousness.

The verse right before it is also very tough-as-nails-sounding. Music aficianados will recognize that this is a *Messiah* song too, performed as a bass solo. Notice:

But who may abide the day of His coming? and who shall stand when He appeareth? for He is like a refiner's fire, and like fullers' soap.

This is pretty brutal stuff! It sounds so out of character, as we picture Almighty God in heaven, beating on someone like a blacksmith, plunging the precious metal into the fire over and over to drive out all the impurities. Maybe He sends trials and hardships, or allows the Devil to pour on the temptations. "And he shall *purify* the sons of Levi. He will purge them as gold and silver, so that they can offer unto God an offering in righteousness."

And yet this is undeniably part of the picture. God loves; He accepts; He redeems. But then He also purifies those who are His. All through the history of God's dealing with His people, He has chastened and rebuked and mentored and purified. I can still remember taking a translated praise hymn over to Bangkok for a week of spiritual emphasis. The Thai word for "purify" is *chamrah*–an essential expression as we sang together: "Purify my heart; let me be as gold and precious silver. Refiner's fire; my heart's one desire is to be holy, set apart for You, Lord." Then in the concluding verse: "Purify my heart; cleanse me from my sin–deep within."

However, let me share the testimony of so many people who drive home through L.A.'s twinkling Christmas lights after the Sing-Along Messiah. We're glad for *all* that the Messiah is! I'm thankful that our Savior, Jesus Christ, is . . . Wonderful, Counselor, the Mighty God, the Everlasting Father, the Prince of Peace. And yes, I'm glad that He's also a Purifier. I'm glad that He's willing to rescue me from sin–based on Calvary–and that He's then willing to take my life and transform it.

What kind of December message would Christianity provide if it couldn't change our lives? Even through hardship, aren't you glad that God makes Himself responsible for remaking us, for turning us into the beautiful, holy creatures He had in His mind during the Creation?

I confess to a bit of holiday schizophrenia as I read through the theological observations of C. S. Lewis. (Speaking of Fishamblestreet and the foggy streets and grand concert halls of that corner of the world.) But I concede with considerable Protestant consternation that Lewis believed in at least a sanitized form of *Purgatory*!

That's right. He was a champion of evangelical Christianity, a proclaimer of grace that is freely given. And yet, as he examined his own life, shortly before his conversion, he found himself becoming aware of his own desperate sinfulness. "For the first time I examined myself with a seriously practical purpose. And there I found what appalled me; a zoo of lusts, a bedlam of ambitions, a nursery of fears, a harem of fondled hatreds. My name was legion."[1] Mortified and ashamed of his own craven soul, he had a desire to be cleansed. He had this conviction that even after death, he would stand before God in his filthy rags, his yet unperfected character, his mixed motives . . . and want for God to bring out a hose and a character scrub brush of some kind.

In *Letters to Malcolm,* he blurts out the inexpressible this way: "Our souls *demand* Purgatory, don't they? Would it not break the heart if God said to us, 'It is true, my son, that your breath smells and your rags drip with mud and slime, but we are charitable here and no one will upbraid you with these things, nor draw away from you. Enter into the joy'? Should we not reply, 'With submission, sir, and if there is no objection, I'd rather be cleaned first.' 'It may hurt, you know'–'Even so, sir.'"[2]

Well, the ways of a holy and divine God in bringing us to completion and purity are a mystery we can never fully plumb. My church does not believe in the flames of purgatory and neither do I. But here's a second slice of wisdom from the same author . . .

I love how C. S. Lewis, in his book *Mere Christianity*, gives more practical encouragement to those of us who, yes, may have great impurities in our lives: "If you are a poor creature–poisoned by a wretched up-bringing in some house full of vulgar jealousies and senseless quarrels–saddled, by no choice of your own, with some loathsome sexual perversion –nagged day in and day out by an inferiority complex that makes you snap at your best friends–*do not despair*. He knows all about it. You are one of the poor whom He blessed. He knows what a wretched machine you are trying to drive. *Keep on.* Do what you can. One day (perhaps in another world, but perhaps far sooner than that) He will fling it on the scrap-heap and give you a new one. And then you may astonish us all–not least your-self: for you have learned your driving in a hard school. (Some of the last will be first and some of the first will be last.)"[3]

Isn't that beautiful? The purifying blows come from a Father's loving heart.

Maybe you remember that verse in Matthew 7 where Jesus asks: "If your son asks you for bread, would any of you dads give him a stone?" And a lot of times we look up at God and we say, "Hey! You DID give me a stone! What is this? I scraped my knuckles on it! This stone You threw at me hit me in the head!"

But you know, we learn later that what maybe hurt so much *was* actually bread. It was what we needed to nourish and transform us during a hard time. In the end, it is always bread.

Back now to Mrs. Susannah Cibber, singing in that very first performance of the *Messiah*. A talented singer who, ironically, could not read music, Handel himself painstakingly taught her the vocal parts. Three years earlier, we read in the history books, this woman was disgraced in a sex scandal that culminated in a trial which revealed the adulterous relationship forced upon her by her husband, Theophilus Cibber, the son of the theater manager. For three years Mrs. Cibber had been persecuted and pained; she'd been through the refiner's fire. And now she sang the contralto solo about the suffering of Jesus: "He was despised and rejected, a Man of sorrows and acquainted with grief."

As she finished, and the last notes died away, Dr. Patrick Delany, chancellor of St. Patrick's Cathedral, stood up and cried out, "Woman, for all this thy sins be forgiven thee." The sacrifice of the Savior was sufficient to purify all sins; forgiveness and redemption *were* possible.

And that has been the message of the *Messiah* for more than 250 years.

Behold, a virgin shall conceive, and bear a Son, and shall call his name EMMANUEL, God with us. Isaiah 7:14, Matthew 1:23

5

Behold! A Virgin Shall Conceive

There's a cheerfully earthy joke shared in *A New Song,* one of Jan Karon's delightful books about Father Tim Cavanaugh and the nice people who live in the fictional town of Mitford. Uncle Billy Watson, who enjoys the spotlight, has a penchant for knee-slappers. "Wellsir, this census taker, he went to a house an' knocked, don't you know. A woman come out, 'e said, 'How many children you got, an' what're their ages?'

"She said, 'Let's see, there's th' twins Sally and Billy, they're eighteen. And th' twins Seth an' Beth, they're sixteen. And th' twins Penny an' Jenny, they're fourteen–'

"Feller says, 'Hold on! Did you git twins ever' time?'

"Woman says, 'Law, no, they was hundreds of times we didn't git nothin'.'"[1]

• • • • •

Song #8 is one of the shortest little pieces in all of Handel's *Messiah.*

It's a recitative for the alto soloist, and it runs only about thirty-five seconds. Just the title is almost the whole song. "Behold! A Virgin Shall Conceive."

That's taken from two passages of Scripture: Isaiah 7:14, and then Matthew chapter one, which is basically quoting back from Isaiah. But here's the whole verse as written by this Old Testament prophet some seven hundred years before a baby Boy in Bethlehem was given the name Jesus.

Therefore the Lord Himself shall give you a sign; Behold, a virgin shall conceive, and bear a Son, and shall call His name Immanuel. In Matthew, the Bible writer adds the footnote after "Immanuel": . . . *which being interpreted is, God with us.*

There's a very fundamental question facing us two thousand years later as we listen to this song and as we ponder the mysteries of what Christians call the Incarnation. Here it is–and any street-wise nine-year-old these days can point us to the dilemma. *Virgins don't conceive!*

Babies arrive on this planet according to a certain process, and they don't come at all to persons in a state of virginity. Everybody today knows this, and everybody in the year 4 B.C. knew it too. If you stay right in Matthew one and read verses 18 and 19, you discover that Joseph, Mary's fiancé, knew this. Virgins don't conceive. They just don't. There's a certain IF-THEN timeline which governs this process of pregnancy and childbirth, and if his beloved Mary was pregnant, then he and the whole world knew what must have happened earlier. According to Uncle Billy, *A* may not lead to *B,* but it's a stark reality that *B* was always preceded by *A*.

We can really ask two tough questions about it all. First of all, why would God do things this way? Why a virgin? And then–putting it simply–do we believe it? Do we buy this once-in-a-lifetime story? Does it matter?

If we stay with Isaiah, we discover at least part of God's motivation immediately. *The Lord Himself shall give you a sign.* Here's a Baby going to be born, and if we accept the Word of God as truth, it's born in a different way than all other babies. I wasn't born this way, and neither were you, and neither are our children. But one Baby, if the Bible is telling the truth, was born of a virgin. Just this one time a virgin did conceive. Is that a sign to us? As I continue leafing through my *Messiah* score, let me tell you right now: *I accept it as being one.*

In both the Matthew and Luke accounts of this miracle, we discover even more. The virgin Mary didn't just conceive all by herself; the Word of God tells us that the Holy Spirit moved upon her. The Holy Spirit was in a very real sense the Father of this Child. Jesus Christ, born as a Baby with real flesh and blood and vernix and placenta and a newborn's wrinkled skin and all the rest, was at the same moment a divine Being. He was God there in that manger; He was conceived through the power of the Holy Spirit.

Now, the theology of this is much too deep to solve in a brief Christmas book. But I believe the Bible when it tells us that a virgin conceived and that this is a miracle designed to be a sign to us, to give us confidence that God has intervened on this planet. We can know that this was a different birth, that something galactically significant and otherworldly took place in Bethlehem.

But now to the second question. And people are asking it bluntly these days: do you believe it? Do you buy this story? We all have brains, the critics say. We've all been to biology class. We've all picked up the facts of life from somewhere. We all know that virgins don't conceive; they just don't. And then they ask: why in the world would you believe that it happened this way here?

You've probably heard of the name Bishop John Shelby Spong, a theologian who has been in the news in recent years. His book, *Why Christianity Must Change Or Die*, was a real stunner, and he makes a couple of startling assertions. Number one, he says, Jesus' mother, Mary, was not a virgin. No way. Number two, in his opinion, the marriage feast at Cana where Jesus turned water into wine was Jesus' own wedding. Jesus Himself got married that day. In his earlier book, *Rescuing the Bible From Fundamentalism*, he also asserts that the Apostle Paul was a homosexual, so we have here a trilogy of challenges to the Christian faith.

"'He was conceived by the power of the Holy Spirit and born of the Virgin Mary,'" Spong writes. "Certainly if that phrase is to be understood literally, it violates everything we know about biology. Do we not yet recognize that all virgin birth tales–and there have been many in human history–are legendary? They are human attempts to suggest that humanity alone did not have the ability to produce a life like the one being described. All virgin birth stories, including the ones about Jesus, were fully discredited as biological truths by the discovery in 1724 of the existence of an egg cell."[2]

So there's a growing army who are red-inking the Virgin Birth out of their Bibles. Russell Shorto, writing for the secular magazine *GQ*, short for *Gentlemen's Quarterly*, did a major piece in June of 1994, reporting on a scholarly group called the Jesus Seminar. And he poses the question in this article which, very appropriately, is entitled "Crossfire."

"What happens when some of the world's leading scholars of Christianity agree that the man behind the religion was just a man?" He goes on: "He wasn't born in Bethlehem (Nazareth is more likely), his mother wasn't a virgin, he didn't come back from the dead, and he never fancied himself a divine being."

This panel of theologians known as the Jesus Seminar has essentially dismissed approximately 80% of everything Jesus Christ ever said. And here as reported by this writer in *GQ*, they eliminate the virgin birth, the resurrection, and just about everything else.

C. S. Lewis addresses the modern reality that many people, including Christians–and including theologians–begin their study of the Bible with one debilitating caveat firmly in view: *miracles do not happen.*

If someone is healed, it must have been medicine. If people crossed the Red Sea, the tides must have been only six inches deep. If an axhead floats, it was probably made of foam rubber. If someone rose from the dead, all the observers standing around must have fallen into a collective trance. And if a virgin has a baby, she's lying. Because biology textbooks *don't* lie and miracles never happen.

Well, what do we do with this? Can we trust our own Bibles?

The critics pick apart Isaiah 7:14, quoted above, and they correctly point out that the Hebrew word *'almah* is uncertain in its meaning, but that it generally means "young woman," with the specific connotation of being able to bear a child, sexually mature. The Hebrew word *bethulah*, which Isaiah could easily have used and didn't, is much more precise in meaning "virgin."

However, in the New Testament, Matthew 1:23, where the Bible writer Matthew quotes from Isaiah, what Greek word does he use? Here it is: *parthenos*, which means very strictly: "virgin" with the full and explicit definition of sexual purity that we understand today. Of course, the critics and the Bible scholars in this Jesus Seminar group and others like it immediately suggest that Matthew simply compounds what they call the mis-translation of Isaiah. "Isaiah simply meant 'young woman,'" they conclude, and Matthew turned an error into a full-fledged pillar of the Christian faith. "And, lo, a tradition was born," scoffs one.

But I don't believe that argument holds up, and all you have to do is to read the rest of Matthew 1 or Luke 1. In Matthew you don't just have the word "virgin" there in verse 23. Verse 18 says explicitly:

[Jesus'] mother Mary was pledged to be married to Joseph, but before they came together, *she was found to be with child through the Holy Spirit.* Then verse 20, and this is God's own messenger angel speaking: *"Joseph son of David, do not be afraid to take Mary home as your wife, because what is conceived in her is from the Holy Spirit."* Verse 25: *"He [Joseph] had no union with her until she gave birth to a Son."*

If you study the parallel passage in Luke one, this great Bible writer actually quotes Mary's conversation with the angel Gabriel. And in verse 34, Mary herself asks: *"How will this be . . . since I am a virgin?" "How shall this be, seeing I know not a man?"* is how the more subdued King James Version puts it.

And then the same answer comes back again, upholding this great Bible truth. Luke 1:35, and let's stay with the beauty of the King James: *And the angel answered and said unto her, The Holy Ghost shall come upon thee, and the power of the Highest shall overshadow thee: therefore also that holy thing which shall be born of thee shall be called the Son of God.*

Well, there we have it. And you and I have a couple of choices. We can say to ourselves and to each other, "There's no such thing as miracles. Babies aren't born of virgins; that's never happened, we've never seen it happen, and that's the end of it." We could decide that even God Himself doesn't have the power to cause this to take place, as a sign or as a miracle, or so that He Himself would be the Father of this Baby or for any other reason.

Keep in mind, though, that we would have to accept some other things while rejecting the Virgin Birth. Out with the Virgin Birth and IN with the realization, then, that Matthew 1 contains one, two, three, four blatant lies. Four out-and-out falsehoods. In Luke 1, go through and count them for yourself. Four more lies . . . and one of them spoken by Mary, the mother of Jesus. "How can this be, since I'm a virgin?"

In his book *The Jesus I Never Knew*, Philip Yancey recalls a TV episode of *Thirtysomething*, where a character named Michael argues with his wife at Christmastime:

"Do you really believe an angel appeared to some teenage girl who then got pregnant without ever having sex and traveled on horseback to Bethlehem where she spent the night in a barn and had a baby who turned out to be the Savior of the world?"[3]

End of quote. End of diatribe. And do you know something? That's exactly what I *do* believe. I want to believe my Bible; I want Jesus Christ to be "that holy Thing." At this very moment in time, I'd gladly and willingly and openly stake my life, my eternal life, on that exact scenario, on the 35-second testimony of a song which is our greatest hope today.

O thou that tellest good tidings to Zion, get thee up into the high mountain; O thou that tellest good tidings to Jerusalem, lift up thy voice with strength; lift it up, be not afraid; say unto the cities of Judah, Behold your God! Arise, shine, for thy light is come, and the glory of the Lord is risen upon thee. Isaiah 40:9

6

O Thou That Tellest Good Tidings To Zion

In that same book, *The Jesus I Never Knew*, Yancey describes a couple of heartbreaking personal stories. A Christian youth pastor discovers that his wife and infant daughter both have AIDS. Soon he's going to be left alone because of the brutally random bad luck of that one tainted blood transfusion. One pint of bad blood! And this young man, knowing that the cemetery is soon going to claim his two most precious treasures, writes to Yancey and asks: "Where is God?"

Story Number Two. Another man, dedicated Christian who happens to be blind, opens up his home to a recovering drug addict. "You can stay here with us," he tells the visitor, trying to follow the example of Jesus. Weeks later he discovers that this person is having an affair with his own wife, right there under his own roof. And in the blackness of his own blind heartache, he cries out too: "Where is God?"[1]

Well, there's a song–and a Bible passage–that eloquently answers that cry leaping from seven billion throats on this one rage-infected planet: "Where is God?"

"O Thou That Tellest Good Tidings to Zion" also comes out of Handel's well-used Isaiah chapter 40. I mentioned earlier how the first 39 chapters of Isaiah are filled with denunciations and pronouncements of judgments: sin and sorrow and mistakes and maledictions and doom and destruction. No wonder the faithful few of Israel joined today's generation in weeping through their persecutions, "Where is God?"

But then for 27 chapters, beginning with this beautiful Isaiah 40, the author looks nearly a millennium into the future and writes about a Redeemer. Exactly what visions of a cradle and a cross heaven showed this messenger we don't know in all the details, but chapter 40 signals the beginnings of hope. Even before you turn on the music, listen to verse 9's spectacular announcement:

O Zion, that bringest good tidings, get thee up into the high mountains; O Jerusalem, that bringest good tidings, lift up thy voice with strength; lift it up, be not afraid; say unto the cities of Judah, BEHOLD YOUR GOD.

And to a world that's been crying out for thousands of years about the absence of God, about the unanswered prayers and the triumphs of the wicked and the taunts of the Philistines and "Why did my child die in that car crash?" and the holocausts of World War II and Rwanda and September 11, 2001, here comes the answer in this one verse. "Behold your God." "Look in a manger in Bethlehem," God tells the world through His servant Isaiah. "See the Baby? That's God."

And then for thirty-three years the real Messiah walked on this earth. He worked and got tired and sweat and bled with us. And He was the God we could SEE.

"What difference did Jesus make?" asks Yancey in another volume. "Both for God and for us, He made possible an *intimacy* that had never before existed. In the Old Testament, Israelites who touched the sacred

Ark of the Covenant fell down dead; but people who touched Jesus, the Son of God in flesh, came away healed. To Jews who would not pronounce or even spell out the letters in God's name, Jesus taught a new way of addressing God: ABBA, or 'Daddy.' In Jesus, God came close."[2]

Philip Yancey goes on in his book to observe that there were at least three times when even Jesus cried. Just like us, He cried at a funeral–before He raised His friend Lazarus to life. He cried over the city of Jerusalem, knowing that this was a city even God couldn't rescue. And in Hebrews He ". . . offered up . . . loud cries and tears to the One who could save Him from death."[3]

And despite the healings that Jesus performed, the miracles, the resurrections, the crowds fed, the Bible only records a total of approximately thirty-six miracles. Even God Himself, walking those dusty roads, was able to rescue so few. People just in the next village over missed the miraculous moment, the supernatural blessings–and so even God wept over the futility of having to wait. Even God, a bearded Man with sandals and twelve followers, despaired that there were problems He couldn't fix *yet*.

But this was God! Our anguish was His too; He shared our tears. Waiting for God's final movements, God's ultimate triumph, was just as difficult for Him as it is for us; in fact, a million times harder because His love for the human race was so intense. But in His tears and His despair on the cross and even in His eventual cry of triumph, we see the eagerness of God to rescue all of us. As we look at the Messiah predicted and promised by Isaiah, we truly can "Behold OUR God."

"Because of Jesus," Yancey adds in his book, *Disappointment With God*, "we no longer have to wonder how God feels or what He is like. When in doubt, we can look at Jesus to correct our blurry vision."[4]

I think there's one prayer we should never pray, at Christmas or any other time. And it's this: "God, please show us Yourself." Because He's already done that–with the most eloquent, most clearly stated demonstration He could ever give: His own Son. Do you long for a clear picture of God right now, as you read and think about this? The clearest picture has already been sent to this planet! God can't outdo what He already did. All He can say to us is what Isaiah said to a confused and searching nation of Israel: "Behold your God."

Maybe the musicians among us have wondered what motivated George Frederick Handel. He was a well-paid man who enjoyed the patronage of people like King George the First and the Duke of Chandos. His anthem "Zadok the Priest" has been played at all British coronations since that of George II. So fame or financial rewards certainly weren't the primary forces driving him.

I believe in my heart that this unique composer had an intense desire to take those sheets of paper and, much like the Bible prophet of old, write something that would give the world courage. "Behold your God." For twenty-four furious days and nights he set down those notes to match Scripture's inspired lyrics so that we could listen this December and behold our God. "I think I did see all Heaven before me, and the great God Himself," he wrote. May that be our Christmas experience as well.

For unto us a Child is born, unto us a Son is given, and the government shall be upon His shoulder; and His name shall be called Wonderful, Counsellor, the Mighty God, the Everlasting Father, the Prince of Peace. Isaiah 9:6

7

For Unto Us a Child Is Born

I have a very thought-provoking but tongue-in-cheek political Christmas question to ask you today. How would you feel about all of us getting together and repealing the 22nd Amendment to the United States Constitution?

If we did, that would mean that any president, instead of just being limited to serving at most two terms, could have five or six or even ten terms. He could keep going until the year 2058–if he could keep getting the votes.

I can imagine a good number of you flinging this book against the nearest wall at the very idea of a Donald Trump or Barack Obama settling in for two decades at 1600 Pennsylvania Avenue. Or a Texan named George W. Bush. In the 1990s, many diehard "broken glass Republicans" ("I'd crawl over broken glass to get Slick Willie out of there!") would have turned purple at the thought of their political archrival escaping the political clutches of Lewinsky-gate and winning a third term.

On the other hand, back in 1988, more than a few loyal Republicans wished longingly that President Reagan could extend his stay in Washington. They'd have given just about anything to have the Gipper in command there for twelve years instead of eight.

Well, they always say there is no passion like political passion, and I try to stay away from such topics; even some of my in-laws look at me askance when I pull up at family reunions with a certain type of bumper sticker on my Camry. But as we get to Song #12 in Handel's *Messiah*, I find a truly intriguing biblical proposal being made.

"For Unto Us a Child Is Born" is taken entirely from Isaiah 9:6, and I think this is one of the grandest pieces in the entire oratorio.

For unto us a Child is born, unto us a Son is given, and the government shall be upon His shoulder: and His name shall be called Wonderful, Counsellor, the Mighty God, the Everlasting Father, the Prince of Peace.

There are a couple of soul-stirring Christmas points for us to discover, and also some good news regarding the 22nd Amendment. But notice, first of all, that this Child is born "unto *us*." Maybe you've read a birth announcement where a son or a daughter is born *to* Mr. and Mrs. Jones. That little baby is born *into* their family; he belongs to them. He comes into that home as a full-fledged family member, and is there to bring gladness and joy and fulfillment. I recently jumped onto Facebook and cheerfully announced that twins–a granddaughter and a long-awaited grandson, Audrey and Miles–had been born *unto us.* Even just as a grandpa living five hundred miles away, I glowingly accepted praise and compliments and handshakes and good wishes and vegetarian chocolate cigars and all the rest. Oh that shall be . . . glory for *me.* You bet.

And here our Savior, Jesus Christ, is born "unto us." What a beautiful Christmas thought! But there's more, as we notice in the very next line: *Unto us a Son is* given.

In the book *Love in a Distant Land,* Pastor Mike speaks to a group of Buddhist high school students. After giving a respectful moment of appreciation to the devout faith of their own upbringing, he goes on to make the point that Jesus was God's gift to everyone. Jesus isn't an American deity, a western God. The United States doesn't own the patent on Jesus. God gave His own Son as a King who offers to die and redeem high school kids living in all corners of the globe.

So a Son is *given.* Have you ever thought about that? Jesus Christ, the Baby in the manger, the Lamb of God, the Savior, Immanuel–"God with us"–was *given.* Someone gave Him.

The little reference note for Isaiah 9:6 in my NIV study Bible sends me straight over to a certain verse in the New Testament. Right where Isaiah uses the word "given," the marginal reference says something that you and I would certainly expect: "See John 3:16."

Have you ever noticed? *For God so loved the world that He* gave *His only begotten Son.*

Think about what a gift that was! To give your own Son, to say goodbye to your Son for a 33-year journey to a faraway planet in rebellion. Jesus didn't have to go, and God didn't have to give Him. And when we consider the kind of love that exists between God the Father and God the Son–well, we can't even comprehend this gift. We can sing about it, but we can't understand it.

And now consider this too. The song tells us that "the government shall be upon His shoulder." The government of the universe will rest upon the strong shoulders of the triumphant King, Jesus Christ.

How do we feel about that? Every time we elect a U.S. President, many of us wonder: "Is this man up to the challenge? Can he carry the load?" And during every single four-year term, many, many Americans begin to say to themselves: "Nope. Here in this 21st century, the job's just too much. He can't do it." Whether it's a Richard or a Gerald, a Ron, somebody named Bush, a Bill, a Barack, a Donald. In the 2012 campaign, it was a constant refrain of candidate Mitt Romney: "Obama's a nice guy–he's just not up to the task. He's in over his head. Etc." We don't always ascribe any real sinister or resentful feelings to our conclusion; we simply decide that the man or woman wasn't big enough for the job. The levers of power and the load of responsibility are just too much for a mortal man to bear.

But here the kingdom of the *universe* will rest upon the shoulder of Jesus. Is He qualified? Can He do it? Jesus Himself said to His followers in Matthew 28:18, just before returning to heaven: *"All authority in heaven and on earth has been given to Me."*

So, just as the prophet Isaiah predicted, and just as George Frederick Handel set to music back in 1741, Jesus has already got the job. Is He up to it?

Well, the rest of this single *Messiah* verse, Isaiah 9:6, answers the question beautifully. What are the attributes of this new King? List them again. "Wonderful. Counselor. The mighty God. The Everlasting Father. The Prince of Peace."

That's a pretty good resumé, isn't it? I notice in the New International Version, that instead of separating "Wonderful" and "Counselor," they put those together: a "Wonderful Counselor." And that's okay too. A wonderful Counselor is a good thing; together or separate, these are attributes we're glad our King has.

We could stop for a long celebration about every single one of these five character traits, but why don't we simply look at that last one: "Prince of Peace"? Especially in December, our hearts immediately go to the book of Luke, chapter 2, where the angels sang: "Glory to God in the highest, and on earth *peace*, goodwill to men."

The coming of this Messiah was to bring peace to mankind, peace to troubled hearts. And peace to you and to me.

Later in the book of Isaiah, over in chapter 53, also featured in Handel's oratorio, we find this very interesting expression: "He was wounded for our transgressions; He was bruised for our iniquities; the chastisement of our *peace* was upon Him." In the New International Version, we find it described this way: "The punishment that *brought us peace* was upon Him."

This is Bible truth: the punishment that came to Jesus brings US peace! How? That's the story of the ages; that's the message in its totality of Handel's *Messiah*: how the agony of Calvary–the agony that Someone else bore–brings us peace today. Knowing that all condemnation has been canceled, our fate reversed, we can face our future with confidence and lasting peace.

Finally, just before the orchestra begins, let me ask you: *If* a leader, a president, came along who was perfect . . . wouldn't you want him or her to stay on? If our president truly was a wonderful counselor, mighty and wise and caring and strong–we'd want that 22nd Amendment repealed! We'd long to have that perfect, capable, loving Leader forever! We'd want Him to be "an *everlasting* Father." We would march in the streets in order to keep Him forever. Demolish the voting booths and shred the ballots, we would exult. We are done with the frustrating agony of hesitating between two flawed and limited and self-serving choices.

That's why I want to shout for joy when I read the prophet Isaiah's very next verse. After that marvelous list of Christ's attributes, it says this: *Of the increase of His government and peace,* there will be no end! *He will reign on David's throne and over his kingdom, establishing and upholding it with justice and righteousness from that time on and forever.*

No more election days! No way! Not ever again! Not when we get Jesus Christ for our everlasting King.

Glory to God in the highest, and peace on earth, good will towards men. Luke 2:14

8

Glory to God

In an old, old Charlie Brown comic strip from at least a generation ago, Linus just isn't able to memorize his Christmas lines from Luke 2. You know: *And it came to pass in those days, that there went out a decree from Caesar Augustus, that all the world should be taxed.*

After some of his stumbling around and procrastinating and pouting into his blanket and complaining about how hard his part is, older sister Lucy sticks her fist in his face and tells him there are five good reasons why he's going to learn that part RIGHT NOW, sucker! And then she spreads out her hand to show him those menacing five fingers: "One, two, three, four, five" . . . and then than iron Lucy Van Pelt fist once again. And boy, instantly he knows his part and can pretty much recite all 52 verses of Luke chapter 2 in King James English, Hebrew, Greek, Swahili, whatever you want. And then he looks into the camera and observes,

"Christmas isn't just too commercial, it's getting too dangerous!"

And right there in the very heart of Luke 2, in Linus' assigned speech, there's a verse that speaks to us about danger and fear. There's an expression that shows up several times in the Bible, and frankly, it's almost a bit amusing to read. In three of the Gospels, when Jesus walks on water, the disciples are sure they're seeing a ghost out there on the waves. And Jesus calls out to them: *"It is I; be not afraid."*

In Matthew and Mark, He says it this way: *"Be of good cheer: it is I; be not afraid."*

And now here in Luke 2, as we read through the story where shepherds are out in the fields with their flocks late at night, a huge apparition appears in the midnight sky.

The angel of the Lord came upon them, and the glory of the Lord shone round about them, and they were sore afraid. "Terrified," adds the NIV.

Now, I don't know exactly what happens in the midnight sky when the "glory of the Lord shines all around," but it's got to be a supernatural, other-worldly, scary experience. And we've all seen pictures of enormous angel beings; they radiate intense light and have swords of vengeance strapped to their sides. And people looking on are definitely "sore afraid."

Then in verse 10, the angel says the two words that almost make us smile.

"Fear not."

I've got to tell you something. If I was out in the desert, and suddenly saw the sky filled with the awesome sight of the glory of the Lord, and then a being of fire and light, an angel from God's throne, said to me: "Fear not" . . . do you know what I'd be tempted to reply? I think I'd say, "Listen, Mr. Angel, I'll fear if I want to! You can say whatever you like–I'M SCARED!"

But the good news from Handel's *Messiah* is this. Those two words, "Fear not," are the very heart of the Christmas message. To a world that was terrified of God, to people who were scared of heaven and distrusting of the deity and convinced God was their worst enemy, this angel came down to tell those shepherds God's message. Those two words, "Fear not," are God's message to the world–both in the year 4 B.C. and now again today.

Notice that just four verses later, the skies are really filled now with an angel choir. And here are the lyrics, quoted verbatim, from the song they traveled here to sing: *"Glory to God in the highest, and on earth peace, good will toward men."*

"His favor rests on men," says another version. But the unfolding Christmas drama is the ultimate story of reaching out, of saying, "I love you. Please don't be afraid of Me anymore."

In Handel's original manuscripts, he penned in for this song: "Da lontano e un poco piano," meaning "As from a distance, and rather *softly.*" Even the composer wanted this angel chorus to bring peace, not overwhelming fear.

I've appreciated many spiritual nuggets from Philip Yancey's book, *The Jesus I Never Knew*. And even that title has something to say to us, doesn't it? A God we didn't know, the strange God we didn't really trust, reached down with His best gift and said through an angel choir, "Don't be afraid; it's Me."

In his chapter on the incarnation, Yancey writes: "Unimaginably, the Maker of all things shrank down, down, down, so small as to become an ovum, a single fertilized egg barely visible to the naked eye, an egg that would divide and redivide until a fetus took shape, enlarging cell by cell inside a nervous teenager."[1]

He goes on to observe that all through the Old Testament, there were certainly images of fear. God was thunder and a burning bush; He was earthquakes rolling down from Mount Sinai. He touched Jacob's thigh and the man was instantly crippled. Plagues brought death and destruction from heaven itself. No wonder the Jewish nation expected their Messiah to come relentlessly across the desert like an unstoppable, conquering army.

But no. God said instead, "Fear not." He came as a baby so that we would "fear not." "God made a surprise appearance as a baby in a manger," Yancey observes. "What can be less scary than a newborn with his limbs wrapped tight against his body? In Jesus, God found a way of relating to human beings that did not involve fear."

Well, that's very touching, you say . . . but what about *me*? Can you hear God saying right now to YOU–yes, you–"Fear not"? I don't know your name, but He does. It's a personal reaching out: "John, Phil, Nancy, Lynn, Juan, Katrina, Kenji . . . fear not. Don't be afraid of Me." And then that angel chorus, with its personalized verse written and composed and rehearsed and sung just *for* you and *to* you: "On earth, peace; good will toward you." Today, this very moment, cutting through all the Christmas clatter and the jingling bells, comes the message of God's angels: that His will for you is good.

Then shall the eyes of the blind be opened, and the ear of the deaf unstopped; then shall the lame man leap as an hart, and the tongue of the dumb shall sing. Isaiah 35:5, 6

9

Then Shall the Eyes of the Blind Be Opened

If you've ever seen the play, "The Miracle Worker," you know a little something about this story of a blind, deaf, and mute child named Helen Keller, and her teacher, Miss Sullivan. There's this incredible breakthrough moment where little Helen suddenly realizes that her world is filled with THINGS, and that there are words which in her mind can tie to those things. Those five, strange hand-shapes that this nameless person in the dark had always pressed into her palm–W-A-T-E-R–stood for water! That wet stuff splashing down on her. That was water. And this soft thing was D-O-L-L, "doll," and those cool blades of . . . *something* were G-R-A-S-S, "grass." And this face, this kind face with the wet streaks on the cheeks–that was T-E-A-C-H-E-R. "Teacher." It's a wonderful story, a moving moment.

But as we continue this Christmas journey through the *Messiah*, there's another moment coming which is even better, more to be anticipated. It takes the alto soloist exactly twenty-nine seconds to sing this tiny solo, but it's going to take Jesus even less time than that to accomplish what the prophet Isaiah prophesies for us in chapter 35, verses 5 and 6.

Then shall the eyes of the blind be opened, and the ears of the deaf unstopped. Then shall the lame man leap as an hart, and the tongue of the dumb shall sing: for in the wilderness shall waters break out, and streams in the desert.

I guess we just plain and simple cannot imagine what it will be like when *instantly*, in the twinkling of an eye, nobody is sick anymore. Blind people–instantly seeing. Deaf people–instantly hearing, taking in the resurrection blast of the trumpet of God and the throbbing anthems of the angel choir. Crippled people leaping for joy, break-dancing on the abandoned graves of those who have come forth to new life. People who couldn't say a word here in this life will suddenly lift up their hands and lift up their voices and sing, shout, scream, cry, rejoice over the miracle that's just happened to them.

Only once in a while, our God does give us just a glimpse. It's been two thousand years since the Christmas baby came down to this world, already ripped apart by illness. And He did grow up to be a Man and He went around for three-and-a-half years healing a few people in one country. But that's been a long time. Our memories have grown dim, and so have our hopes. All the more reason to treasure stories like this one, borrowed from the late Pastor Adrian Rogers' book, *Expect a Miracle But Believe In Jesus*.

He tells about a friend named Marolyn Ford, who was blind just like the people living in Galilee and Judea. She and her husband prayed and prayed and prayed about it, but her eyesight worsened until she was completely blind. And then one night, they had this special feeling like they should pray again. Just like that, she could see perfectly! Instantly! She was 20-20. And she wrote in her book, *These Blind Eyes Now See*, "We wanted to run down the street at one a.m. and shout that I was blind, but now I see!"[1]

And that miracle's going to happen a million times over. Instantly, in the twinkling of an eye, all God's people will see again, sing again, hear again, run again, and especially, live again.

But I do wish that the prophet Isaiah and George Frederick Handel had added just one more ailment to this list: the blind, the deaf, the lame, the mute. They'll all celebrate, for sure, and their loved ones with them. But I think of many families around this globe where someone so precious has been developmentally disabled. People used to say "retarded," and that hurt so much. But they were! An enemy of boys and girls had stepped in and retarded their growth, what they could do or think or understand.

We all have these people we know. I have a cousin who gave birth to the most beautiful baby. They were enthralled, crazy in love with the God-sent gift. But it didn't take long before they realized that something was terribly wrong. This innocent child was never going to have abilities extending much beyond those of maybe a two-year-old. I imagine most of us could tell a similar story.

These wonderful Christians, crushed as they were, determined to love this child, protect her. By God's grace, they would care for her as long as she lived. They had a second child, and I can hardly imagine the anxious moment there before they realized that he was completely well and normal.

But years went by, and this little girl became a teenager. Her body, of course, was a teenager's body. Everything happened to her that would happen to any other young woman. Can you imagine the confusion, the fear, for her when those monthly cycles first began? She had no idea what this was. And her mom and dad could never explain the beautiful mysteries of womanhood, what it might mean for her someday, that this was part of God's incredible and perfect design. They couldn't tell her they loved her when cramps hit, when hormones flooded through her.

And the last time I visited my cousins, I came away thinking about this moment promised in the Word of God. True, deaf people will hear. Lame people will leap around like happy rabbits. But what about kids like my niece? I'll tell you something–in an INSTANT, they will suddenly stand up straight and tall, with eyes that gleam with new intelligence. Suddenly they'll *know*! Suddenly they'll understand! All at once the words "I love you" will not be just noise, but words of comforting joy. She will hear the angel choir and understand the words as they're sung.

Maybe you remember that television character from quite a while ago, "Benny," on the program *L.A. Law*. Just mildly disabled, but life was always so hard. He had a little job sorting papers and stapling them and taking out the trash, but there was always the fog of confusion, of not "getting" things, of not comprehending. And then, when Jesus comes, people like Benny and my cousin's daughter will immediately, miraculously, have all the wires–which once were crossed or disconnected –perfectly fixed in just one moment.

And one more thought about this day of miracles. Because what happened to this beautiful girl was the deliberate work of a sinister someone. It was no accident, and somebody named Lucifer exulted when that "mistake" happened. He stands there in the delivery room, hissing in quiet, demonic delight when a cord cuts off oxygen, when chromosomes are out of place. He sees our tears . . . and he laughs! He brings on blindness, and then chuckles to himself. It makes me think of the story Jesus told, with the good Farmer who looks out over the fields where suddenly there are weeds which bring pain and destruction. He says quietly: "An enemy has done this." And He plans for the future day when He will solve that problem.

The last time I was out on the camp meeting trail, I preached a sermon where, all at once, I could hardly speak with the emotion of it: "I look forward to the day when my little niece will be well . . . *and the devil will be destroyed*!!" Don't you agree? There really is going to be a payback time–not that we have to engineer it. God is fully capable of settling all accounts. Blind people will see, sick people will be well, those hit with the curse of this mental darkness will see the light . . . and a being named Lucifer, along with his armies, will feel the flames of God's own lake of fire.

Maybe life is so perfect where you live that this promise, this 29-second song, doesn't mean that much. You have 20-20 vision already, two good legs, and a nice bank account. Just a few chapters earlier, though, this same Bible writer tells us that we *all* need the miracle of Resurrection Morning. Here's Isaiah 6:9, 10: *He [God] said, "Then go and give My people this message: No matter how much you listen to Me, you do not understand. You matter how much you look, you can't see what's happening to you. Your hearts have become so scarred by sin that you no longer sense what's good, and your ears are so deafened by worldly sounds that you no longer hear what I'm trying to tell you. You don't want to see, to hear or to understand because you don't want to change and be healed."*

Well, here's one sinner who wants his eyes fixed. And ears and mind and heart.

And before you hit "PLAY" to hear this 29-second masterpiece, let me add one thing. Sometimes people have surgery, or take medicine, and it works . . . but just for a while. And families are devastated when they hear the five terrible words: "The tumor has grown back." But not here! Not on this wonderful day. There will be no temporary miracles when Jesus comes again. The eyes He'll touch will be well forever; the minds He heals will never be confused again. The hearts He mends will never hate or hurt, ever again in God's glorious universe.

He shall feed His flock like a shepherd; and He shall gather the lambs with His arm, and carry them in His bosom, and gently lead those that are with young. Come unto Him, all ye that labor and are heavy laden, and He shall give you rest. Take His yoke upon you, and learn of Him; for He is meek and lowly of heart: and ye shall find rest unto your souls. Isaiah 40:11, Matthew 11:28, 29

10

He Shall Feed His Flock

A new demographic category has been revealing itself here in the United States during recent presidential elections. Have you noticed how "SOCCER MOMS" are the new sought-after group, the prize voting segment the Republicans, Democrats, and Tea Partyers are now courting? "We're interested in your needs," their Facebook ads say. "We know how hard you work to hold down an eight-to-five job, and then still run a household and get your kids to music lessons and sleepovers and especially to soccer practice."

Time Magazine once ran a cover story on these women who have this driving concern for their kids. No pun intended as we think about all the SUV mileage soccer moms put in taking their children to all of the necessary and all of the enriching activities of life. A crossover hit, "Hats," by Christian artist Amy Grant laments how soccer moms have to fill so many roles, supply so many needs, keep so many people happy all the time. How can she work all day, then all night, being both a mom and a lover? "Working for a livin', all because I'm driven." Etc. Etc. And then the signature line of soccer moms everywhere: *Why do I have to wear so many hats?*

Well, as our *Messiah* MP3 player continues to spin out God's Christmas message, another unforgettable slice, from the Bible, we almost find mention of soccer moms here too. And really, it's in a song, and a Bible passage, where maybe you never noticed it before.

Song #20 in George Frederick Handel's masterpiece is a double solo, first for an alto, and then a soprano. (A "shout-out," as they say, to my dear Arroyo Grande friend, Mary Bishop, who hit those high notes so beautifully even when she was several months pregnant!) "He Shall Feed His Flock Like a Shepherd." And once again, Handel takes his inspiration from the beautiful 40th chapter of Isaiah.

He shall feed His flock like a shepherd, and He shall gather the lambs with His arm, and carry them in His bosom, and gently lead those that are with young.

We could spend many months considering how Jesus is like a shepherd to us. All through the Psalms, and here in Isaiah, and then in Matthew 11, where the second half of this song is completed by the soprano: *Come unto Him, all ye that labor and are heavy laden, and He will give you rest. Take His yoke upon you, and learn of Him, for He is meek and lowly of heart, and ye shall find rest unto your souls.*

That's a beautiful Christmas message. But especially during the frantic, mall-packed shopping weeks before Christmas, let's stay with that motif of soccer moms. It's so beautiful how we're promised a Savior who gently leads those who are with young. Moms with kids. Parents who care about the spiritual nurturing of their sons and their daughters. Single dads who find it hard to pick out presents for their five-year-old girl.

My older daughter, Kami, just gave birth to those twins I mentioned earlier. Born at just 26½ weeks, they had to stay in the NICU for nearly four months. When they finally went home, Kami's days were quickly swamped and overwhelmed by the fatiguing daily grind of bottles and feeding and diapering and pumping and rocking . . . all times two. It sometimes felt, I'm sure, like the duties of motherhood were two *squared,* that she was coping with a quadruple burden. But Jesus promises to gently lead those that are with young.

The text notes for this Bible passage direct us all the way back to the book of Genesis, chapter 33, where Jacob and his estranged brother Esau have just had a meeting where they're reconciled. It's a beautiful moment, and then Esau says, "Let's continue our journey. I'll go with you; I'll accompany you."

And his younger brother, with all the flocks and herds and many, many kids in his tribe, says this: "My lord knows that the children are tender and that I must care for the ewes and cows that are nursing their young. If they are driven hard just one day, all the animals will die. So let my lord go on ahead of his servant, while I move along *slowly* at the pace of the droves before me and that of the children."

Jacob felt keenly his responsibility to all of the young, to the tender ones under his care. And these precious lines of Scripture, set now to music, "He Shall Feed His Flock," should encourage every struggling person who is courageously taking care of their young. As you care for your children, Jesus promises to care for YOU. As the prophet Isaiah writes, the Good Shepherd promises to gently lead you as you lead the treasures God has given to you.

Sometimes we're desperate to have someone help us, to almost carry us. Especially at Christmas time, maybe, when your arms and your soul are so filled with packages–maybe you're still carrying a toddler, even–and you just want to say, "Lord, I need someone to carry *me* for a while here." And God promises us in Isaiah 40 that He'll do that.

In the inspirational film *Shadowlands* there's a poignant scene where

Christian writer C. S. Lewis has just lost his wife, Joy. And he's absolutely crushed with grief, so filled with despair. He wants to hibernate, to withdraw from his friends, and be alone with his self-pitying tears. But there's his stepson, Douglas, just a boy, also numb with loneliness and sorrow that he's lost his mom to cancer. And finally Jack Lewis' brother, Warnie, says to him: "*Talk* to Douglas; he's just a boy. You've got to help him." So up in the attic, there's that Oscar-worthy scene where this middle-aged writer and the young boy, both filled with spiritual doubts and overwhelming anguish, talk and cry together. C. S. Lewis, strong Christian that he always thought he was, when it was time to help his boy, needed God to help *him.* And in the end, a loving God did indeed provide that strength.

So, soccer dads and soccer moms, take heart because the strong Shepherd is especially there to help you. I love how E. G. White, in the 19th-century book *The Desire of Ages*, describes how much Jesus cares about our needs.

"Christ is as verily a personal Savior today as when He lived a man among men. He is as verily the helper of mothers today as when He gathered the little ones to His arms in Judea. The children of our hearths are as much the purchase of His blood as were the children of long ago. Jesus knows the burden of every mother's heart. He who had a mother that struggled with poverty and privation sympathizes with every mother in her labors. . . . In every grief and every need He will give comfort and help."[1]

Do you want to claim the promise of some of that comfort and help right now? Why not whisper a prayer and ask for some at this very moment as the music plays?

His yoke is easy, and His burthen is light. Matthew 11:30

11

His Yoke Is Easy, and His Burthen Is Light

Okay, get ready, because here's the hardest musical song in the entire oratorio! This one really moves along, and it's got the sopranos' highest note: a B-flat. Our friend Handel has moved to the New Testament, and this beautiful verse in Matthew 11:30:

His yoke is easy, His burthen is light.

Jesus, of course, is the one to actually make this statement in Scripture, so it reads: "*My* yoke is easy and *My* burthen–or burden–is light." (Interestingly, Handel and his librettist, Charles Jennens, made the entire project "third-person.") This verse follows the soccer-mom invitation we just considered: *"Come unto Me, all ye that labor and are heavy laden, and I will give you rest. Take My yoke upon you, and learn of Me; for I am meek and lowly in heart: and ye shall find rest unto your souls."*

But now, with all due respect to Mr. George Frederick Handel and to a disciple named Matthew–and maybe even to our Savior Himself–we have to ask this probing question: IS IT? Is the yoke of Jesus *easy*? "Burthen" is an old-fashioned word, but is the burden of the Christian faith a light one to carry? Or is it a ten-ton package?

It's interesting to note, in digging into the old Greek meanings, that the word *chrēstos*, translated in the Bible as "easy," actually has a more subtle nuance. For example: "fit for use." In fact, in the Living Bible, which is an excellent paraphrase, verse 30 is rendered this way: "Wear My yoke–*for it fits perfectly*–and let Me teach you."

In other Bible passages, *chrēstos* is translated as "good," "kindly," or "pleasant." Not *easy* in the sense of something not being difficult. So is it more the case that the yoke of God is good for us to wear, like spinach is good for the diet, instead of easy?

A couple of absolutely breathtaking illustrations come to us from the Fall 1996 issue of *Leadership* magazine, which is a resource I appreciate more and more all the time. Quoting from *The Pastor's Update*, May 1996, published by the Foreign Mission Board of the Southern Baptist Convention, there's a story about a Pastor Jack Hinton of North Carolina, who was leading worship at a leper colony on the island of Tobago in the West Indies. As he took requests from the people, there was just time for one more song. And a lady who'd kind of been facing away from the pulpit turned around and raised her hand.

Hinton recalled later, "It was the most hideous face I'd ever seen. This woman's nose and ears were entirely gone. The disease had destroyed her lips as well. She lifted a fingerless hand in the air and asked, 'Can we sing . . . "Count Your Many Blessings"?'"

And that moment just ripped at the heart of Pastor Hinton. How could this woman, this leper, who had experienced nothing but tragedy, nothing but disfiguring and the disapproval of society, with her flesh eaten away by a disease that couldn't be cured . . . how could she want to sing "Count Your Many Blessings"? How could she possibly think that Christ's yoke for her was an easy one?

Hinton was so overcome by emotion that he simply had to leave the sanctuary. Outside, he was struggling to regain his composure when a fellow team member said to him, "Well, Jack, I guess you'll never be able to sing that song again." And Hinton finally looked up at him, tears still in his eyes, and told him: "Yes, I will, but I'll never sing it the same way."

Here was a woman who trusted so much in her God that to her, the burden was light. A leper–and her burden was light. To me that's just unbelievable faith.

There is a Christmas trilogy of ways that Jesus' yoke can be an easy one for us. First of all, just as He did for His listeners there by Galilee, He offers us grace. Do we live existences bound down by rules and regulations and codes and codicils? Is our religious life straitjacketed by legalism? Those Jesus came to serve were being choked by a religious life that was weighted down by the rules, by manmade observances and traditions. And Jesus came down from heaven to say to them, "No! Come to Me; I'll give you rest. My yoke is easy; My burden is light." No wonder a grateful disciple named John wrote years later in his first epistle: *His commands are not burdensome* (5:3).

And maybe Christmas is a good time to rediscover Christ's gift of grace. (All other times are good too!) Again, going back to *Leadership* magazine and its priceless page of quotes, Jerry Bridges offers this from his book, *The Discipline of Grace*: "Your worst days are never so bad that you are beyond the *reach* of God's grace. Your best days are never so good that you are beyond the *need* of God's grace."

I guess that covers all of us, doesn't it?

Here's application #2. Maybe there are things in this world you and I don't fully comprehend. We're confused by theology and by the turmoil of mixed-up world events. Political trends don't go like we wish they would; things are a mess at the office, and we want to just cry out: "I DON'T UNDERSTAND!!"

There's an interesting sound bite that comes from William Wordsworth, English poet, who wrote on the topic of contentment. And he actually includes that old-fashioned word "burthen"–which is how I found this quote: "CONTENTMENT: That blessed mood in which the *burthen* of the mystery, in which the heavy and the weary weight of all this unintelligible world is lightened."

Are you confused and mystified by this old world and the way it's groaning down into oblivion? Why not give that up to Jesus? A previous *Messiah* song describes how Jesus, the mighty God, will have the government "upon His shoulder." Take hold of that assuring guarantee. And then you and I can have our burden lightened; we can experience full contentment.

Here's a third pathway to peace. Maybe you're a person who's driven to succeed; you have a reputation as a doer. In the past twelve months you've accomplished more than anyone else on the payroll, and it looks like another fast-track year is coming up.

But all those expectations are a tremendous burden. People expect fourteen hours a day from you! If you leave the office before 9:00 p.m., somebody wants to know why. Your parents and your spouse and your kids and even your dog are always on your case: "Why don't you live up to what you *ought* to be able to do?" Like the cartoon character Linus once shouted to the skies: "There's no bigger burden than a great potential!"

And who knew more about that than a composer named George Frederick Handel? Talk about high expectations! Even kings expected miracles from him every single opera season; could the maestro of the court top last year's performance? In fact, U.S. poet Ralph Waldo Emerson once did an essay entitled "Art" for the book, *Society and Solitude*, and he defined "wisdom" like this:

"Raphael paints wisdom, Phidias carves it, Shakespeare writes it, Wren builds it, Columbus sails it, Luther preaches it, Washington arms it, Watt mechanizes it . . . Handel sings it."

On the one hand, you might say, that's very, very nice. On the other hand, talk about a pedestal! Talk about peer pressure! But even to Handel, maybe especially to Handel, victim of such high expectations, the Prince of *Peace* beckons at Christmas time.

"Come unto Me . . . My yoke is easy, and my burden is light."

Together with a relieved and grateful composer named George, let's celebrate God's gift of burden-lifting grace.

Behold the Lamb of God, that taketh away the sins of the world.
John 1:29

12

Behold the Lamb of God

It's interesting that even though this book began as a holiday radio series running through four successive Decembers (with this chapter's segment airing all around the world on Christmas Day a few years ago,) Handel's *Messiah* actually has two parts to it. And it's worth noting that "Behold the Lamb of God" comes right after the so-called Christmas section. There are some very Bethlehem-flavored songs like "For Unto Us a Child Is Born," "There Were Shepherds Abiding in the Field," and "Glory to God." But then there's usually an intermission, followed immediately by this song, #22, "Behold the Lamb of God."

I get a very real sense here that Handel is saying to us, even here as we close out another year, "All right, Christmas has come and gone. The Baby-in-a-manger part is over. The wrapping paper has been put away. And NOW, what are you going to do about this Man, this Lamb of God?" And every Christmas Day, as a man or woman looks to the future, that is the most important question we can pose: "What will you do about this

Lamb of God?" I still recall a praise song from a couple of decades ago, where the singer very plaintively has God asking: "What have you done with My Son?"

Speaking of Christmas mornings, in the year 1943 Roosevelt delivered one of his famous fireside chats. World War II was going on, and the President talked very frankly about *looking at* the destruction of war, the casualties. Part of what he said: "The war is now reaching the stage when we shall have to look forward to large casualty lists–dead, wounded and missing. War entails just that. There is no easy road to victory. And the end is not yet in sight."

In essence he was telling a war-torn world: "This is what we face. There will be death. Look at it hard. Even on Christmas Day, the news is stark and sobering. There will be dead bodies lying in the snow before this is all over." And he reminded us all to behold the pain, the sacrifice, that would make everyone free again.

If you ever get the chance in Washington, D.C. to visit the FDR exhibit, by all means, do so. It's an incredible, moving sight, with quiet water fountains, and this strong, silent statue of a crippled man, who once told us we had nothing to fear but fear itself. And carved on the brick walls as you move about the exhibit are excerpts from some of his most important speeches. Perhaps you've heard the one which he gave in Chautaqua, New York, on August 14, 1936. Again we get this sense of *looking*, of staring directly into the eyes of death, of the destruction caused by evil.

"I have seen war," he says. "I have seen war on land and sea. I have seen blood running from the wounded. I have seen the dead in the mud. I have seen cities destroyed. I have seen children starving. I have seen the agony of mothers and wives." And then these three quiet words: "I . . . HATE . . . WAR."

Here in this most important of *Messiah* songs we find the entreaty of heaven itself, spoken through John the Baptist in John 1:29: *The next day*

John saw Jesus coming toward him, and said, "Behold! The Lamb of God who takes away the sin of the world!" (NKJV)

Perhaps there's no better Christmas present–good all 365 days of the year–than the biblical advice found in those five words: "Behold the Lamb of God." Stop whatever you're doing and look. Turn off the TV and look. Set aside your pile of presents for fifteen minutes and look. Look at Him. Think about Him . . . not so much regarding the mangers and the carols, but what He did for you as the *Lamb* of God. If we glide through our December 25s, gleefully opening our presents and singing carols and eating pie and watching twinkling lights, but don't behold the Lamb of God, then we're the most foolish people in the universe. Because God is reaching out to us with His own Fireside Chat, telling us: "I hate war. I hate sin. I hate death. So please . . . look. Behold the Lamb of God."

Roger Bullard points us to the musical fact that this song is slow . . . but not despairing. Rather, the grandly ponderous chorus hints at "the inexorability of divine determination. This is the focus of the line suggesting laboriousness: 'that taketh away'–now a pause, almost as if for rest, 'the sin of the world,' the line rising higher, depicting the heavy weight of sin being lifted from the world by Messiah's agony. The melody shapes itself to the divine task."[1]

During the years that I wrote radio sermons for Christian radio, and now continue to reflect on the beauty of the gospel message, this is a continuing urgent message: "Behold the Lamb of God." I hope these few pages serve the purpose of adding to John the Baptist's invitation: "Look over here! Look at who's coming down the road toward the River Jordan. It's Jesus. And He's the Lamb who takes away the sin of the world."

Surely He hath borne our griefs, and carried our sorrows; He was wounded for our transgressions; He was bruised for our iniquities; the chastisement of our peace was upon Him. Isaiah 53:4, 5

13

Surely He Hath Borne Our Griefs

I can still remember the tightening in my heart when a frantic call came from an Ojai friend. Ken, one of the pillars of our little church in that funky New Age tourist town, had collapsed. Medics were vainly trying to revive him.

I jumped in my car and tore up the mountain road to the small community hospital, but before I got there this giant of a man had passed to his rest. I comforted his bride, held her hand as we prayed together, and made phone calls to some of the key church members.

That weekend we all grieved and hoped together, looking forward with steadfast confidence to the day when Christ would call our friend forth to a new and eternal life.

And I still recall one of the points from that long-ago funeral homily. Because this generous and saintly man knew how to carry the loads of others. I confessed to his wife that I was almost afraid to clear my throat around Ken and say, "Wouldn't it be nice to have this or that?", because the next weekend, *voila!*, that new wireless microphone or new DVD player would be installed at the church, all hooked up and ready to go. I had to be careful not to say to Ken something as innocuous as: "My Camry has a rattle in it"; I was afraid he'd go get me a new one. This dear man seemed to know that when you take care of the shepherd, you take care of the sheep. And Ken took care of Pastor Dave to a fault.

But Ken, burden-bearer that we all knew him to be, was simply following the example of his Master and Lord. And one of my favorite *Messiah* songs takes us directly to the lonely hill of Golgotha in a poignant reminder of what Jesus does for us.

Surely He hath borne our griefs and carried our sorrows. Every Christmas, Lisa and I go to an elegant place where people are all dressed up, and we join in a performance of *Messiah.* We drive there in a comfortable car with a good heater for the cold December air. We pay ten dollars for parking and pull the money out of a wallet that has lots more where that came from. And then we sing: "Surely He hath borne our griefs and carried our sorrows." And how does this biblical line apply to the loss of my friend Ken?

First, we have the core Christian message that Jesus carried the weight of our sins. Without that, of course, a church family would have no business even considering the hope of a Resurrection. As good and worthy a man as my friend Ken was, he could never qualify for a Resurrection morning in his own strength. Our farewell to Ken would have been a permanent parting, an entering into a void of separation with no end to it.

When the controversial film *The Passion of the* Christ was released a few years ago, *Christianity Today* described how one of the sources used for the movie was a 18th-century Christian named Anne Catherine Emmerich. She envisions a scene in the Garden of Gethsemane where Lucifer confronts Jesus. Is He really going to attempt this impossible thing, to go to Calvary for these lost specimens of humanity? And the serpent hisses at his archenemy: "Takest thou even this sin upon thyself? Art thou willing to bear its penalty? Art thou prepared to satisfy for all these sins?" And Jesus says: "Yes. I'll take the whole thing. I'll carry it all to the Cross." *Behold the Lamb of God who taketh away the sins of the world.*

In addition to the burden of our sins, Jesus also took upon His shoulders the hurt, the suffering, the sorrows of our lives. There are many griefs that He carried, so that we would not have to carry them.

Let's prayerfully reflect on this on two levels. First of all: pure pain. Physical pain. A crown of thorns and the thirty-nine lashes. The blood and the tearing of flesh and the slow asphyxiation of a crucifixion. Jesus bore the worst of the physical pain so that we would not have to face ourselves the real physical pain, the hurt, of lostness and of hell. He carried that sorrow, and the Bible record is starkly plain that, just physically, it hurt enough for Jesus so that any objective observer, any referee from outside the system would say: "That's a fair sacrifice, an appropriate exchange."

But I don't think that's the level Isaiah is talking about. When my own dad was struck down by a hit-and-run driver in 2002, I lay awake in bed that night and my heart was physically hurting. I could feel it like a stone. I could feel the hurt. But the physical hurt was not the tough one to deal with.

No. The hurt that looms so large, and the one Isaiah tells us Jesus will carry for us, and the one that makes me say, "It is good to be a Christian," is the specter of lostness, of eternal separation, of saying goodbye forever. Of everlasting loneliness. Of being in that emergency room and knowing the person who holds all your dreams, everything, your knight in shining armor, your lover and best friend . . . is gone and forever gone.

Many, many people go through that. They put a shovelful of dirt into a grave, and say with a wildly broken heart: "Goodbye forever. I'll never, ever, ever see you again."

And what Jesus carried for us–the greatest burden He lifts from us with Calvary–is this haunting specter of eternal separation from God the

Father and from those we love. He carried that, and now we don't have to.

All through Jesus' ministry, He spoke with confidence about what He and His Father were going to do. He was going to die, and then be resurrected. He said it; He believed it; He proclaimed it. Jesus did not come down here to fail. He knew He was not going to fail.

And yet it seems plain that when He entered into the darkness, the hell, of that last weekend, it got to where Resurrection Sunday–the hope, the confidence, the guaranteed mission–all of that was taken away. The presence of God was withdrawn. The knowledge of reunion was obliterated. And there on the cross, in one horrifying moment, Jesus accepted and carried the reality of separation. For the sacrifice to be complete, Jesus had to feel like a lost sinner who would never go home again, who would never see His Dad again, who would never again feel the love of His family. And He cries out to the empty universe: *My God, My God, why have You forsaken Me?*

And there I think we find the fullness of fulfillment of Isaiah's prophecy. *Surely He hath borne our griefs and carried our sorrows.* Physical pain and blood are not the real thing Jesus carried, Mel Gibson movies notwithstanding. But because Jesus took this sacrifice clear to the limit, experiencing the darkest, blackest midnight of eternal separation, today we do not carry it. Jesus carried it, and now we are free in Him.

We have the joy of reunion, because Jesus carried the burden of no reunion. We have the anticipation of heaven, because Jesus took on Himself the possibility that heaven was forever beyond His reach. My three brothers and I can know we will see our dad again because Jesus was willing to feel as though He never would see His Dad again.

So it is good to be a Christian. It is good to serve a Savior and Friend who once invited us to carry someone else's suitcase for two miles instead of one, and then showed us exactly what He meant by carrying this unbelievable load on our behalf up that hill to the Cross. *Surely He hath borne our griefs and carried our sorrows.*

And Jesus invites us to let Him carry this burden. The burden of our sins. The heavy load of our pains. And most of all, the sorrow of saying goodbye, which He lifts from us by having carried Himself through the tomb and on into light of an everlasting Paradise.

And with His stripes we are healed. Isaiah 53:5

14

And With His Stripes We Are Healed

Comedian Steve Allen brought the house down at a convention of the Religion Communications Congress back in 1990. "They don't write songs the way they used to," he told the Nashville crowd of several thousand writers and PR pros. He then proceeded to read word-for-word the lyrics to a rock-and-roll hit entitled "Satisfaction" by the Rolling Stones. Which, if you remember that particular thumping song, doesn't exactly have the deepest message in the world. It's pretty much– "I can't get no . . . I can't get no . . . I can't get no . . . satisfaction. No, no, no. Hey, hey, hey, that's what I say."

And so on, et cetera. Musicologists have spent very little time through the years analyzing the depth, the thought patterns, the subliminal innuendo and political threads of Mick Jagger's fulminating in that song. And no doubt you and I can remember other songs on the radio from whatever generation that just repeated the same mindless refrain over and over *and over* again. And someone jokes: "I wonder what's the name of THAT one?"

Well, as we keep playing these inspired selections from Handel's *Messiah*, and think to ourselves, "Now there's some music," it's kind of interesting that even composer George Frederick Handel, powdered white wig and all, included a song in his libretto that repeats the same familiar one line a total of *thirty* times! A simple seven-word line, and the sopranos, then the altos, and then the tenors and basses just keep repeated these seven words over and over until they get up to thirty repetitions.

Right in the middle of this classic oratorio, is a special trilogy of songs: numbers 24, 25, and 26. All three of these choruses come from the Old Testament, out of the inspired prophecy of Isaiah, chapter 53. And I want to say right here that Handel can be forgiven for the repetition of Number 25: "And With His Stripes We Are Healed." More on that in a moment.

First, though, here are the three verses where Handel got his lyrics. Isaiah 53:4-6:

Surely He hath borne our griefs, and carried our sorrows: yet we did esteem Him stricken, smitten of God, and afflicted. But He was wounded for our transgressions, He was bruised for our iniquities: the chastisement of our peace was upon Him; and with His stripes we are healed. All we like sheep have gone astray; we have turned every one to his own way; and the Lord hath laid on Him the iniquity of us all.

Every time we read these three verses, I know that music lovers immediately have *Messiah* infuse their minds and their souls. Which is something very precious and almost miraculous about this particular piece of music. There's something intangible about the songs in this oratorio that bring the Bible to life. Of course, the source verses from *Messiah* are found all through the Word of God, from Psalms and Job and Isaiah and the Old Testament prophets like Haggai and Malachi, and then from the Gospels, Romans, Hebrews, and the "Hallelujah Chorus" in the book of Revelation. So *Messiah* aficionados, as they prayerfully read the Bible each day, often have these sudden goosebump moments where tears spring into their eyes–"Yeah, there's another one!"–and the memories of music and deep meaning work together in a kind of spiritual synergy.

But even if you're on the other musical side of the Great Divide and can't tell one note from another (and every song sounds to you like "The Star-Spangled Banner") these three verses in Isaiah are still powerful medicine for us. Because this is the gospel message right here! Notice again: "Surely He hath borne *our* griefs, and carried *our* sorrow."

In the Clear Word paraphrase, it adds: "He *willingly* bore our griefs."

Then in verse five: "He was wounded for *our* transgressions, He was bruised for *our* iniquities: the chastisement of *our* peace was upon *Him*; and with *His* stripes we are healed."

Maybe you hear these verses about the cross and it makes you want to jump ahead to Easter. But as holiday celebrants think at Christmas about gifts, especially undeserved gifts, these verses tell it all. Jesus Christ came down here. He didn't have to, but He did–and He took our stripes, our punishment, the chastising, the crown of thorns we should have gotten, the nails in His hands that should have been in *our* hands, the cross on Calvary that should have said D-A-V-I-D, my name in the nameplate at the top, and yours too. He took all of that for us, and then in its place gave us the gift of eternal life.

Then we come to the wonderfully broken record, and if a song ever had to wear out its groove, this is a most worthy moment for that. Because in Song #25 is that one line Handel repeats thirty times. Over and over again, he reflects the Christmas message of Isaiah 53:5: *And with His stripes we are healed.*

May I humbly say this? I think I need to hear that message thirty times, maybe even a hundred and thirty times. *And with His stripes we are healed.* I just watched a YouTube video of the gospel song that reminds us: "Heartaches–broken people. Ruined lives *are why You died on Calvary.* Your touch is what I longed for. You have given life to me." That says it all.

It's because Jesus came to this planet as a baby and then gave His life for you and for me that we are healed. Gifts and presents and decorated malls and the exhilaration of the cold winter air won't do it; lights and Christmas trees and even Christmas choirs can't heal you. A good sermon next weekend can't heal you; even the happiest Christmas reunion with your family can't heal the wreckage that's in your soul and mine. But the stripes of Jesus, the blood He shed on that cross . . . it heals us. Nothing else in this universe heals except for the stripes that were laid on Jesus. And so I say to the Christmas choir: "Sing it over and over again to me." *And with His stripes we are healed.*

Jesus wasn't born in a manger just to get His picture on Christmas cards. He came here at *Christmas* to do what we celebrate at *Easter*. He came here to go to Calvary and take those stripes, to bear our agonies and then heal us. What a tragedy if we miss the very event that Christmas is meant to lead us to accept!

The history books tell us that Handel, as a 35-year-old musician, established himself as a court composer and conductor in Hannover, Germany. But even before the year was over, he took off for London on an extended leave of absence, leaving behind some unhappy sponsors. A year later, after being back in Hannover for just a short time, he flew the coop a second time, and this time stayed away for years. Now he was really in trouble. Microsoft and Home Depot had intended to drop their logo into all his Christmas specials, and now he was leaving them high and dry.

It was even worse than he thought, because in 1714, three years later, his former employer, the Elector of Hannover, became King George I of

England. And here Handel was right under the new king's nose in downtown London! Talk about trouble!

But a year later, at a royal dinner party on the River Thames in 1715, it's said that Handel performed his famous F major suite from *Water Music*, perhaps his second best piece of all time. And King George I decided to forgive Handel for his flightiness, for his two leaves of absence, to wipe the slate clean and accept this repentant musician again. Handel, of course, went on to write some of the best music ever composed, including *Messiah* in the year 1741.

It's a wonderful thing to be forgiven by the king, isn't it? To be accepted in His royal palace once again, to be restored. And surely that's the message of every Christmas.

All we like sheep have gone astray; we have turned every one to his own way; and the Lord hath laid on Him the iniquity of us all.
Isaiah 53:6

15

All We Like Sheep

This is one of those chapters where I almost want to put on one of those disclaimers you sometimes see on television. "WARNING: do not try this in your own home. These are professionals." Because "All We Like Sheep" is one of the toughest songs in the entire oratorio! Right up until the very end, this one really moves. And then the ending moves too . . . but in a different way. You'll see what I mean.

There's something blunt and rather un-PC about the lyrics to this song, but of course, we can't blame the author of the libretto, Charles Jennens, for the words. They come from the pen of the prophet Isaiah, the 53rd chapter. Verse 6:

All we like sheep have gone astray; we have turned every one of us to his own way; and the Lord hath laid on Him [Christ] the iniquity of us all.

There's not a lot of "I'm OK–You're OK" to be found here. No, writing under inspiration, Isaiah tells us: "We are ALL lost." Every single one of us is like a sheep that's gone down the path to perdition.

Even people who walk in the ways of the Lord and drive to God's house fifty-two weekends a year can get to a place of some self-denial. We're reading our Bibles and paying a full tithe. We sit wide awake in church; maybe we even work for the church. Life is good; we have a steady marriage, good job, sound investments. And it seems like unreality when the Bible says–or when a choir sings–"All we like sheep have gone astray." But this spiritual diagnosis is entirely accurate. Every single citizen of this planet has wandered off course. I have; you have. We all have.

In his autobiography, *Just As I Am*, Billy Graham tells about attending a National Prayer Breakfast at the White House back in 1979. Bishop Sheen, the Catholic host of the TV program, *Life Is Worth Living*, was the featured devotional speaker that day. He was retired by then, in a rather weakened condition, with cardiac problems. But he managed to make his way up to the podium very slowly, with Pastor Graham sending up some prayers on his behalf. "God, help him get through this somehow."

About ten seconds later, Billy Graham was almost sorry he'd prayed that prayer. Because Bishop Sheen looked right over at President Jimmy Carter and his wife Rosalynn. And he started out with these words: "Mr. President . . . *you* are a sinner."

What?! Just like that? "Mr. President, you are a sinner"? Which, of course, he is–during the '76 campaign, he famously admitted to *Playboy* magazine that he had often lusted after women in his heart. So the born-again President from Plains was a bonafide sinner, but you just don't say a thing like that. And the crowd almost expected the Secret Service to walk right up and cart Bishop Sheen away, or at least unplug his microphone. But the aging preacher continued. "Yes, Mr. President, you're a sinner." And then he kind of looked down. "And I am a sinner." Then to all of the dignitaries and senators and reporters sitting there: "We are *all* sinners."[1]

Billy Graham shares that by the next December Bishop Sheen had gone to his rest, but no one there at the White House ever forgot that sermon! And he was right. "All we like sheep have gone astray."

There are really two images we might have of sheep, and as sinners we find ourselves falling into both metaphors. For good or for ill, sheep follow the leader. Where one sheep goes, they all go. And from a Scriptural perspective, when one goes wrong, they all do. Handel's oratorio portrays that reality too: "Since By Man"–one man, that is–"Came Death." One man named Adam sinned, and we all followed him. One misstep sent an entire planet reeling off course.

And yet there's another sense where each of us mindless little lambs goes astray in our own foolish and flawed way. We find our own ditch to tumble into. In fact, Line #2 from this verse is so terribly true. "We have turned every one to his own way."

And really, from childhood, even from infancy, isn't that how it is? How many of us who are parents have heard this coming from very young lips: "No, I can do this my own self"? I can tie my own shoes; I can select my own girlfriend; I can choose my own brand of motorcycle, pick my own poison or drug of choice . . . and I can certainly chart my own destiny. Really, every single person on this planet has looked up at heaven and the Shepherd who dwells there, and said in the immortal words of the late Frank Sinatra: "I'm going to do it my way. Don't bother trying to guide me, because I'm going to turn to my own way. I'm an individualist, and I'm going to do my own unique and self-serving thing . . . just like all the other sheep on this farm."

This is our universal condition. You're not exempt from it, and neither am I. We have all gone wrong, purposefully going off on our own, down our own road. Which is the wrong road. Emily Dickinson, the great American poet, writes about this universal dilemma, how each of us is our own worst foe. "The Soul unto itself is an imperial friend–OR the most agonizing Spy an Enemy could send."

So yes, it's universal. And what irony that here are sheep who think they know better than the Shepherd! It's blunt reality that the sheep never know better than the Shepherd–but we think we do. Until God confronts us with this verse and this song, and we realize it: "Oh. I've gotten lost. I AM on the wrong road."

But there's more than realizing, more than a warning fog horn provided here. I'm eternally grateful for the last line, the final climactic promise of this song. *And the Lord hath laid on Him the iniquity of us all.*

What can we possibly say about that? Seven billion lost sheep on this planet; seven billion rebellious wrong roads taken. Seven billion "turnings away." That's a lot of detours and a lot of smashed-up lives broken on the rocks and washed-out bridges of our misguided adventures. But God lays the totality of all of that on Jesus instead. Every single one of us turned to our own way, but Christ the forgiving Shepherd takes that wicked wandering upon Himself, and bears the price of it for us. What a monumental, unfathomable gift, at Christmas and forever.

The next time you play Track #26, "All We Like Sheep," whatever you do, stay tuned right to the very end.

Lift up your heads, O ye gates; and be ye lift up, ye everlasting doors; and the King of glory shall come in. Who is the King of glory? The Lord strong and mighty, the Lord mighty in battle. Lift up your heads, O ye gates; and be ye lift up, ye everlasting doors; and the King of glory shall come in. Who is the King of glory? The Lord of Hosts, He is the King of glory. Psalm 24:7-10

16

Lift Up Your Heads, O Ye Gates

Just this morning I had an office visit from a student named Sandra. A math test hadn't gone very well, and the results were threatening to blockade her future.

She and four friends stopped by to plead their case–and I will tell you why they found my sympathetic ear. All five of them were American war veterans from the blood-stained sands of Iraq.

They had endured 135° heat, going out on patrols in full battle gear, riding in closed-up armored vehicles that could explode over an IED at any moment. Patrols had shot at them. Rockets had whizzed past their heads, missing them by scant inches. Time and again, they had put their lives on the line so that my four grandchildren could grow up in a more peaceful world.

As I always do, I looked in their eyes and said simply: "Thanks, you guys, for serving our country. Thank you for the risks; thank you for the devotion; thank you for winning. Thank you for what your unselfish deeds did for me and those I love, for the secure future you have helped to build."

I was reminded of some of the memorable stories in Tom Brokaw's heralded masterpiece, *The Greatest Generation.* Some of those who served the cause of liberty in World War II really do deserve a parade of glory when they come home. Brokaw's own mom happened to be at the hairdresser's on June 6, 1944, the very day our brave troops were storming the beaches of Normandy. The young beautician who waited on Mrs. Brokaw had a fiancé who was a paratrooper; at that exact moment he might be wounded or even KIA–killed in action. German snipers and machine guns had the beaches ringed, blanketed with a killing onslaught of steel. But somehow this fresh-faced boy survived the horrors of D-Day. He later mailed her the parachute and suggested that she sew a wedding dress out of it![1]

Daniel Inouye, an American of Japanese ancestry, was a commanding lieutenant who served on the front lines in Italy during that same war. While charging up a hill, he was hit by a bullet that punctured his abdomen. He kept going. A grenade flew through the air and exploded right in front of him, shattering his right arm. He kept up the charge, giving left-handed covering fire for his men as they withdrew to a safer position. Another bullet struck him in the leg, but by then his men were safe. He came back home and eventually became a United States senator, serving nine terms before passing to an honorable rest in December of 2012. When first sworn in, then-Speaker Sam Rayburn told the incoming freshmen: "Raise your right hand and repeat after me . . ." Inouye, of course, had lost his right hand on the battlefield, and no one objected when he raised his left instead.[2]

Perhaps the most moving visual image is of men who endure such privations–the cold, the blood, the carnage and terror of being blown to bits–and then finally are able to sail home through the welcoming waters of New York Harbor and see the glowing torch of Lady Liberty. To take a transport train back to Kansas and see the flags and the welcome-home signs. Mom and Dad are there with proud smiles. Mom dabs at her eyes with a handkerchief. A pretty girl who promised to wait through the long months of war flings her arms around the hero's neck and gives him a kiss that makes up for the years of separation. Then the quiet, satisfying ride home to the little white house where dreams can now be rebuilt and a satisfying future explored, free from the scourge of Nazi tyranny.

Welcome home!

There's a line from 19th-century Congregational minister Henry Ward Beecher which goes like this: "Victories that are cheap are cheap. Those only are worth having which come as the result of hard fighting."

And toward the end of the great saga which is Handel's *Messiah*, there is a scene reminiscent of a hard-fought battle and a sweet victory. He takes as his source material the book of Psalms, chapter 24, verses 7-10.

Lift up your heads, O ye gates; and be ye lifted up, ye everlasting doors; and the King of glory shall come in. Who is this King of glory? The Lord strong and mighty, the Lord mighty in battle. Lift up your heads, O ye gates; even lift them up, ye everlasting doors; and the King of glory shall come in. Who is this King of glory? The Lord of hosts, He is the King of glory.

Right there you might have thought my record player got stuck yet again! But this is simply quoting from King David the psalmist, and he repeats the question and answer twice too. What kind of psalm is this?

If we go back into biblical history and study this period of David's reign, we discover that Psalm 24 was actually written and composed to be used as an anthem of military triumph. It's the soundtrack for a parade. The Adventist Bible commentary notes: "David had captured the Jebusite stronghold of Zion and now determined to bring the ark from its temporary resting place in the house of Obed-edom at Kirjath-jearim to the tent that he had prepared for it in the city of Jerusalem. Accordingly, he arranged a ceremony for the occasion in which Psalm 24 was sung as part of the high ritual."[3]

The New International Version text notes for this magnificent Psalm help us to glimpse a double application here. The returning king might be David from this military campaign to rescue the ark of God. Or the king might be the Lord Himself who has successfully brought His people all the way from Egypt to their permanent home in Jerusalem.

In any event, verses 7 to 10 constitute a very special kind of "Who goes there?" The keepers of the gate issue the challenge–a friendly challenge, to be sure: "Who is this King of glory?" The answer comes back from the great choir accompanying the army and the returning King: "The Lord strong and mighty, the Lord mighty in battle." In fact, King David might have arranged, as part of this triumphant ritual, to have two choirs: one to give the challenge and the other to issue the antiphonal response.

So consider that first request: "Lift up your heads, O ye gates. And be lifted up, you everlasting doors." Perhaps it's simply a grand and glorious way of saying, "Open the door!"

Or, and this is just a thought, maybe this was a royal way of proclaiming, "Even the gates of the city are joining in! They're lifting up their heads in worship and thanksgiving. The walls themselves, the fortresses, the gates, the pillars, right down to the stones in the street . . . are all rejoicing that the King is home."

Here's even a third application. In the days of the ancient Olympic Games of Greece, when a victorious athlete would return home to his native land, his home city, the citizens would do something quite unusual. Back in those days, of course, with barbarians and marauders and warfare all around, city gates were locked up tight. But with the champ back in town, the celebrating people would go out to the wall and actually knock a hole in it. They'd whack a big man-sized hole in their wall, deliberately, as if to say: "Our hero is back–so back off! He's our defender! We have nothing to fear. Why should we worry about enemies and their feeble, puny, insignificant attacks? We have our champion back at last!" And maybe King David's song echoes that as well. "Lift up your heads, O ye gates. Lift up the doors! Who needs gates and doors and bolts and double-bolts? The King is coming in! Our Shield and Defender is home!" What a beautiful thought.

Here's yet another scenario. And the Bible doesn't explicitly say this–but I would ask you: why not? As Jesus returned to heaven after His successful mission to Calvary, as He approached the City of God, His former kingdom home, with those battle scars in His hands and feet and a very real wound right there in His side, isn't it possible that angel choirs sang this very song to welcome their King home?

The great war is over. Jesus has defeated Lucifer. Now, after a military campaign that had run a long, bloody, bruising, agonizing thirty-three years, the King is returning. And there are perhaps two uncountable angel choirs with all the parts: soprano, alto, tenor, bass. Millions of singers in the two groups. And the first great choir–they're with King Jesus–issues the challenge: "Lift up the gates!"

The response comes back: "Who goes there?" Actually: "Who is this King of glory?" The angel hosts know the answer, of course; they've been eagerly waiting thirty-three years to sing this song. But they love to ask anyway. And the wonderful answer comes: "King Jesus! The Lord strong and mighty." (He certainly is, isn't He?) "The Lord mighty in battle."

And then, as Isaiah paints the futuristic picture for our consideration, the same question comes again. "Who IS this King of glory?" Every angel can hardly stand the tension now, but they love to ask the question again and again: "Who goes there?" Because it's the most glorious answer in the universe. "Our Jesus is home at last!" They must go back and forth with it a hundred times before the greatest military parade in the history of the universe finally culminates there in the holy City of God.

And what about us? Is there a gate you need to swing open today? Have you had some walls this past year that kept Jesus out? Oh, maybe you let Him partway into your city; you allowed Him a short visit to touch just parts of your life. But not everything. Not every part. Not full surrender. Can you hear the vast angel choir singing to you and to me right now: “Lift up your heads, O ye gates. Lift up the doors. Sweep away the obstructions. Make way, right now, for the King to finally and fully reign in your life”? And the choir doesn’t get tired of singing it, but isn’t it time, right now, today, for our answer?

HALLELUJAH! for the Lord God omnipotent reigneth. The kingdom of this world is become the kingdom of our Lord, and of His Christ: and He shall reign for ever and ever. KING OF KINGS, AND LORD OF LORDS, HALLELUJAH! Revelation 19:6, 11:15, 19:16

17

Hallelujah!

Now at the age of sixty-two, I've sat in front of a TV set for quite a few cliffhanger American elections. Some states quickly pop up blue; the networks color the other ones red. In recent contests, the entire election has sometimes hinged on just a few votes out of a fiftieth and final holdout state, the last ballots or chads which will swing a nation in a different and optimistic but uncharted election.

There have been elections where my candidate lost and I trudged upstairs to bed in a bit of a funk. (Including quite recently.) But once in a while, I've followed the entire process closely, right from the summer debates preceding the Iowa caucuses down to the 8:00 PST poll closings where the troika of California-Oregon-Washington might tip the scales toward a clear winner. And right at that magical hour, every network has proclaimed the glorious news: Candidate X has triumphed! He (or she) has won! There will be parades and celebrations and millions thronging the Capitol and a wonderful, snow-capped day in January when the new leader who carries my hopes and patriotic ambitions, will set their hand on the Bible and then hopefully do great things.

Hallelujah!

Back to our songbooks. Down at Los Angeles' Dorothy Chandler Pavilion, they used to have a delightful tradition. The orchestra and audience would do Handel's entire oratorio straight through, including the "Hallelujah Chorus," and then at the very end, after "Worthy Is the Lamb" and the final "Amen" Chorus, they always did the "Hallelujah Chorus" a second time. I mean, always–with no one complaining. They *always* did it twice, and any conductor that ever suggested varying from that routine would probably have found some tar and feathers on his tuxedo before the evening was over.

But right now, before we turn on our iPods and enjoy that great climactic chorus, I'd like for us to pause and thank our Heavenly Father for a man named George Frederick Handel. You've probably seen old black-and-white paintings of him; he looks very imperious and almost unapproachable with his white powdered wig and his lacy coat with the high linen collar. But for three-and-a-half weeks back in 1741, a real man named George bent over his desk, writing furiously. And in the album liner notes of my own recording, it says this: "The manuscript of the composition shows that Handel could scarcely commit his inspirations to paper with sufficient speed; he drew his pen with impetuous fury through blots and smears."

In fact, the published Schirmer's Edition of "The Messiah" reproduces one of those original pages, from the song "Glory to God." And it *is* a mess, with blotches and notes crossed out. But contained within that scribbling is two things: a revelation of pure musical genius . . . AND the very heart of the Gospel story.

How did this mortal man, this very real flesh-and-blood human, the son of a barber-surgeon, accomplish such a thing? Part of it is that genius, that unbelievable raw talent. Handel was a young musician who, at the age of eighteen, was already the organist at the Cathedral of Moritzburg in Germany. By the time he was nineteen, he'd already written a major work entitled "The Passion According to St. John." Moving to London, he was the music master to the royal family. A fellow you may have heard of, named Ludwig–that's Ludwig van Beethoven, of course–made this confession: "To him I bend the knee, for Handel is the greatest, ablest composer that ever lived."

But this work, the *Messiah*, was something more. There was more here than talent. And virtually everyone who participates in it, whether at a local sing-along, or in a professional capacity, after months of hard practicing, comes to the conclusion that a God in Heaven wanted this music to be written and sung. Somehow, in a mysterious and divinely bathed way, Heaven itself interceded *with* George Frederick Handel, and in those twenty-four days, a miracle happened.

I mentioned earlier how this brilliant composer worked day and night over the *Messiah*, often rejecting the meals his servants brought to him. Sometimes those servants standing outside the door could hear him inside, weeping as he worked, actually sobbing, moved to tears over the saga of the Savior's death and suffering. Handel himself realized that there was a Higher Power at work with him in bringing this oratorio to the world.

Mr. Handel died on an April 14, in the year 1759. During the last several years, he had gone nearly blind. Now the end was near. Eight days before he passed away, on April 6, he did get to hear, one final time, one of his works performed for him. And of course, it was this one: *Messiah.*

And Number 44 in the oratorio, taken from Revelation chapters 11 and 19, is certainly the greatest of them all. *Hallelujah! for the Lord God omnipotent reigneth. The kingdom of this world is become the kingdom of our Lord, and of His Christ: and He shall reign for ever and ever. King of kings and Lord of lords, Hallelujah!*

When you hear that song done live, with the full orchestra and surrounded by the sound of those four musical parts–the sopranos, the altos, tenors, and basses–it comes pounding home to your heart that you're experiencing something that transcends human genius. You are right there in the middle of a kind of divine miracle. In your heart, you know it.

Of course, most of us go to such an event expecting that miracle. We *know* the "Hallelujah Chorus"; we "have our goosebumps ready," so to speak.

But imagine that first time, when the "Hallelujah Chorus" was unveiled. In 1743, when King George II first heard this song, he was so deeply affected that he spontaneously stood to his feet. All his courtiers, following his example, rose as well, along with all the audience, and they remained standing until the chorus ended. Even that first time through, they knew that this was something very special and that they should stand before God. And, of course, for the past 250+ years, we've always stood for the "Hallelujah Chorus." Lisa and I stood together this last Christmas, and what a moment that always is.

But in terms of the White House and CNN debates and posters and ballots, I am certainly ready to say "Hallelujah" to the eternal inauguration of Jesus. I'm prepared to set aside the tradition of blogging and voting, of weighing one platform against another. Wouldn't you like to stand in a very large convention hall–in a kind of galactic Election Central–and see our Redeemer, not on a big screen, but live and in person? Accepting a crown and a throne and the mandate to reign in our lives? *"Forever and ever . . . hallelujah"?*

I know that my Redeemer liveth, and that He shall stand at the latter day upon the earth: And though worms destroy this body, yet in my flesh shall I see God. For now is Christ risen from the dead, the first-fruits of them that sleep. Job 19:25, 26; I Corinthians 15:20

18

I Know That My Redeemer Liveth

It's an expression I heard a few years ago, and these annual pilgrimages to sing Handel's *Messiah* make me think of it. "C & E Christians." Which is short for "Christmas and Easter."

If I were to do a quick guesstimate of the crowd down at the Dorothy Chandler Pavilion here in L.A., there are probably two thousand of us singing the great choruses from that landmark work. And I'm sure that many, perhaps even the majority of those present, are born-again Christians as they participate. So to them, these songs hold significant meaning.

There are others, though, for whom Christmas is simply a sweet, heartwarming holiday. Yes, they accept the fact that there was a baby Jesus and that He was born in a manger in Bethlehem. Yes, He grew to be a man–and said some very memorable kinds of things. That Sermon on the Mount, for instance. They like that. "Turn the other cheek." "Remember the Golden Rule." And at Christmastime, they remember some of the positive contributions that Christian philosophies have made in our civilization.

But here close to the end of the oratorio, please let me tell you something that comes straight from the heart. George Frederick Handel *and* his *Messiah and* the season it all comes packaged in–is so much MORE than Christmas lights and mistletoe and nodding your head to a warm feeling and a few quotable quotes from the Gospels.

As I leaf back through the 252-page musical score for *Messiah*, and simply look at the choruses, I'm struck by the fact that Handel was keying on the most revolutionary, life-altering aspects of the Christian faith. He *focuses* on the Bible passages that seize us by the heart and say: "Listen! This is surrender and repentance! This is the gospel message! Wake up!"

Let's go back through some of these well-known choruses for a reality check. "And the Glory of the Lord Shall Be Revealed." Jesus' coming to earth is an act of *God*, Isaiah says. This isn't just another birth that happens to get onto the cover of Hallmark Christmas cards. This is God in human flesh; this is the beginning of heaven's invasion!

Next chorus: "And He [God] Shall *Purify* the Sons of Levi." The Christmas story is about a U-turn in life, repentance, being cleansed, starting over.

What's next? "For Unto Us a Child Is Born." And then it goes on; Jesus will be called Wonderful, Counselor, the Mighty God, the Everlasting Father, the Prince of Peace. Again, the prophet Isaiah and librettist Charles Jennens and composer George Frederick Handel team up to tell us, This is more than a holiday story! This is the biggest moral turning point in the universe. Jesus is God-on-earth, compelling every man, every woman, every child to make a choice about whether they will have Him as their King of kings and Lord of lords. No wonder C. S. Lewis once observed that an encounter with Jesus is either of paramount importance . . . or not important at all. The one thing Jesus the Messiah cannot be is moderately important.

And then in Part Two: the suffering of Christ. And that's part of the Christmas story too. You take away the Cross and the Resurrection, and what have you got? Basically, you've got nothing. Paul himself wrote decades later, in his first letter to the Corinthians: *If Christ has not been raised, our preaching is useless and so is your faith. . . . If Christ has not been raised, your faith is futile; you are still in your sins* (I Cor. 15:14, 17).

So we have these songs included as well. "Behold the *Lamb* of God." "Surely He Hath Borne our Griefs and Carried Our Sorrows." "And With His Stripes We Are Healed." And then "All We Like Sheep Have Gone Astray," with its powerful ending: "And the Lord hath laid on Him the iniquity of us all."

Let me say again: If we all put on our best suits and our prettiest December evening gowns and go down to that elegant music hall and sing the beautiful music and then walk out to where all the Christmas lights are twinkling in the trees with all those water fountains going, then out to our car in the parking lot and we pull onto to the Golden State Freeway with KOST playing its carols . . . and all we say is, "Well, that was nice. What beautiful music!" well, then, we have tragically *missed* what all this was intended to be. Without Calvary and the Cross and the Resurrection, the baby-in-the-manger story is just a Madison Avenue hoax. That's really all there is to it.

And this song here is one of those that penetrate right to our heart. Yes, it's beautiful; it has the Christmas feel to it. But it still demands of us a response. "I KNOW," cries Job in triumph, "that my Redeemer liveth!" Jesus died and now He lives again. But there's more. In the next verse, and it's in the song, Job proclaims: *"I know that my Redeemer liveth, and that He shall stand at the latter day upon the earth"* (19:25).

Yes, that's a tremendous message, but only if each of us face up to it. Jesus is more than the Christmas baby; He's going to be on this earth again as a returning King, as a Redeemer, and also as a Judge. In other words, this is a story that we have to DO something about more than just sing in December. We have to respond to it; we have to give our lives to it. We have to do something about this *Messiah*.

The last part of the song jumps over to the apostle Paul, who in that same chapter, I Corinthians 15, shouts out in victory: *For now is Christ risen from the dead, the firstfruits of them that sleep* (v. 20).

I don't believe that George Frederick Handel intended that this music ever be simply entertainment, something that takes up one of our holiday evenings. He wanted to confront us with the boldest, most agenda-shattering message of Holy Scripture–and he used his God-given musical talents to do it.

Did you know that Handel is buried in the great Westminster Abbey cathedral in London? Lisa and I have been there, and over his grave is a statue showing the master composer pouring himself into those twenty-four days of feverish, inspired work. And the score he's working on is opened up to this song right here: "I Know That My Redeemer Liveth."

Since by man came death, by man came also the resurrection of the dead. For as in Adam all die, even so in Christ shall all be made alive. I Corinthians 15:21, 22

19

Since By Man Came Death

One man makes a mistake–and an entire planet goes down the tubes. That happened thousands of years ago, and all of us in the first blush of a new millennium still bear the skid marks of that ancient accident. Is that fair? Is that right?

I don't know what your date of birth was, but I do know this: you were born a sinner. You didn't have any choice in the matter. When you emerged into this world, which is a sinFULL world, you were born pre-wired to sin. The software of sin was preloaded in your mainframe before you even got switched on there in the delivery room. Because Adam sinned, you and I today are sinners. Period, case closed. I began a life of enthusiastic sinning on or around the fourth of March, 1955, and have lived in Sin City ever since.

So Song #46 contains some very relevant truth for us way down here sixty centuries after Adam joined the Enemy's rebellion. "Since By Man Came Death" is taken from I Corinthians 15:21, 22. *For since by man came death, by man came also the resurrection of the dead.* Then verse 22 amplifies: *For as in Adam all die, even so in Christ shall all be made alive.*

There's a bit of colossal unfairness lurking here in these two verses. First of all, you and I didn't ask to be born. We're not complaining, mind you, and we think of the comedian's retort to his son: "It's a good thing you didn't ask; I'd have said no!" But we didn't have any choice in being born, and we also didn't have any choice about being sinners. We were born sinners for one simple reason: a man named Adam came along before us and chose to sin. From that one tragic, Edenic moment, every citizen of this planet ever to follow–except for one–inherited that inevitability of sin. Is that unfair? It certainly seems like it. And all because of one man.

Old-time royalty watchers might remember a Christmas surprise back on December 11, 1936, when Edward VIII chose to abdicate the throne of England in order to marry an American divorcée, Mrs. Wallis Simpson. He actually had never been coronated king, but had occupied the throne for about eleven months following the death of his father, King George V. But he made this wrenching decision to step down, so he could "marry the woman I love."

What happened, then, as the result of one man's choice? His younger brother, the Duke of York, became king instead. The left-handed, stuttering sibling–sympathetic hero of Oscar-winner *The King's Speech*–who never expected to be king was abruptly pushed up onto the throne, crowned as King George VI, and he ruled for sixteen years . . . rather effectively as things turned out. He and Queen Elizabeth saw the empire through the bloody days of World War II and the German Blitzkrieg.

But here's the point. Who succeeded to the throne next? Not a child of Edward VIII; no, because of his abdication, his family lost out forever. Instead it was the daughter of younger brother, George VI, a woman we all know as Queen Elizabeth II, who still reigns today. The entire royal family, the line of power, shifted over one place on the family chart. And Elizabeth II is to be followed by her son Charles and then his son Prince William and someday little George and et cetera. Forever as long as the empire shall last, the royal line has been affected for eternity by one man's desire to marry a common American woman.

And such is the nature of sin that it's also passed along. That's a fixed truth as binding as the laws of genetics and family breeding so carefully guarded at Buckingham Palace. There's an interesting little booklet entitled *The Security of Salvation*, written by the late Dr. Richard Nies. He points us to this verse by the Apostle Paul and then assures us that God doesn't blame us for being sinners. Heaven realizes that we were born into sin. In fact, because God created mankind with the capacity for free choice and the ability or possibility of sinning, God Himself actually takes the responsibility for the dilemma the human race is in. "It's My problem, and I'm taking care of it," He announces to the watching universe.

So let's take one more close look at this verse before we turn on the music. Here it is in the Living Bible–and notice heaven's solution: *Death came into this world because of what one man (Adam) did, and it is because of what this other Man (Christ) has done that now there is the resurrection of the dead.* Then Paul goes on: *Everyone dies because all of us are related to Adam, being members of his sinful race, and wherever there is sin, death results. BUT all who are related to Christ will rise again.*

These two brief verses really put the entire question of the universe before us. There are two men, Paul writes. A man named Adam and a Man named Jesus Christ. The deed of Adam those thousands of years ago plunged every single member of his race, the human family, into sin. Now for you and me, that's an involuntary situation. We couldn't help being born into that.

But on the other hand, there is this other Man: the Son of God, Jesus Christ. And four thousand years later, on Calvary, His act of rescue is sufficient to rescue the same planet. The entire human race, damned and doomed by one act, can be redeemed by a second act. But the power, the effectiveness, the applicability of this second act is *not* involuntary. It's not automatic, but it *is* available to everyone who chooses it.

So you can identify–by default–with the first Adam and be lost. Or you can identify–by decision–with the second Adam, Jesus Christ, and be saved. It's as simple as that.

Again, even George Handel himself was subject to the death that Adam's sin caused for all of us. Money or fame or royalties couldn't prevent the ever-encroaching march of the enemy, death, upon him. So near the end of a life no doctor could extend, he sat enthralled as others performed the great *Messiah* choruses he had penned. Eight days later he was gone. "Since by one man . . . all die." Even the great Handel.

And yet the second half of this verse–and this glorious song–are equally true. "Even so in Christ"–one Man–"shall all be made alive." In those last moments of life, that was Handel's hope. And ours.

The trumpet shall sound, and the dead shall be raised incorruptible, and we shall be changed. I Corinthians 15:52, 53

20

The Trumpet Shall Sound

It's one of the most marvelous art demonstrations I've ever seen. Sculptor Alan Collins does something with modeling clay which simply transforms your life. It's called "The Ages of Man." He starts with a clay figure of an infant, a baby boy. And then slowly, shaping a bit here and there, curling in a bit of hair, some more definition to the chin, the baby becomes a little boy, a toddler. He moves a bit more clay around, hardening the cheeks a little. Now he's six, then eight.

Meanwhile, a narrator shares bits of poetry, humor, readings about what it means to be a boy. Then a teenager. Meanwhile, that clay is continually being molded; the boy becomes a man.

And you watch, mesmerized, as Alan is able to add years by simply moving the molecules around. Now he's a middle-aged man; a few wrinkles appear around the eyes. The hairline thins a bit. Flesh sags. The unstoppable effects of age are showing now. Soon he's an older man, still nice-looking, but definitely ready to carry around a card from AARP. Another poem about seeing the leaves fall from the trees.

And now, the music slows down as he's very old. Down to the end, and the shadows of death draw near. And very quietly a bell tolls the marking of the end of life. A cloth is slowly pulled over this old, weary face as the eyes close in death.

But all during the exhibit, which takes about an hour, there's a second figure nearby, also draped. And right at the end . . . is it *really* the end? No! And Alan pulls away the second cloth; a spotlight shines on this new figure, and we see a man in the vitality of youth. Strong, handsome, with eternal life flowing through the veins and immortality written on the face.

And all at once, through the PA system, comes pounding this song from Handel's *Messiah*: "The Trumpet Shall Sound."

Here's a quote which may jolt you a bit, from John Irving's *A Prayer For Owen Meany*. "Anyone can be sentimental about the Nativity; any fool can feel like a Christian at Christmas." That's true, isn't it; even the mall has a Christian feel to it right now. Then he says this: "But Easter is the main event; if you don't believe in the resurrection, *you're not a believer*."

And for most of the month of December, people focus mainly on the soft-and-easy concept of a Baby in a manger. Which is wonderful and good. But the hope of the Christian faith is based on the fact that the Baby became a Teenager just like that clay model. And then a Man. And then a Savior up on a cross. And then three days later, a resurrected Lord and triumphant King. Which is what Handel focuses on in this wonderful song of triumph, taken verbatim from I Corinthians chapter 15, one of the most important passages in the entire Word of God.

Behold, I show you a mystery; We shall not all sleep, but we shall all be changed, In a moment, in the twinkling of an eye, at the last trump: for the trumpet shall sound, and the dead shall be raised incorruptible, and we shall be changed.

I heard a cute bit of humor once, where it was posted on the door of a church nursery. Apparently babies still in diapers don't always cooperate by resting peacefully in there during the pastor's Sunday sermon, because the notice read: "We shall not all sleep . . . but we shall all be changed!"

But all levity aside, that verse holds our only hope for the future. We don't know the timetable, but someday, every one of us will take a trip to the cemetery where we won't be an active or willing participant. We'll be the one they drive in the hearse. And unless Jesus comes first, relatives and friends will sadly say goodbye and lay us in our resting place.

As I edit these words, my three brothers and I are preparing to drive over to a cemetery in Riverside to mark the fifteenth anniversary of my dad's passing. He lived a charmed life as a boy, playing the role of Waldo in the *Our Gang* comedy series. After his conversion, he chose a life of ministry and took all of us to Thailand for seventeen years of colorful mission adventure. But back in 2002, we stood on the sidelines in helpless horror as a drug addict's hit-and-run crime snuffed out Dad's life. And since that moment the flowers have bloomed in the soil above his casket. The sun rises and sets, but he sleeps through it all. Five of his grandkids got married; there are now nine *great*-grandchildren's pictures on the grand piano in Mom's house. But Dad is resting in the arms of Jesus, oblivious to the headlines and the happenings.

But then God promises us that a trumpet will sound! Every believer is going to live again, beginning at that very moment in time. In John 5:25, Jesus Himself promises: *"I tell you the truth, a time is coming and has now come when the dead will hear the voice of the Son of God and those who hear will live."*

But now notice the five words: "And we shall be changed." That old man in the clay modeling demonstration was suddenly new again. Young! Forever young! Forever strong!

A number of years ago, when I was working as a writer for a Christian radio program, I received in the mail one of the kindest, most gracious and thought-provoking letters from an excellent lay scholar in the Catholic faith. She was a lovely, dedicated Christian believer. And she wrote to dialogue with me on the subject of purgatory and its "purgative" effects. I have to say very honestly that she had studied well. She did make a couple of good points and, what's more, they were expressed in the spirit of Jesus.

We already considered the Catholic/Protestant dispute about purgetory in Chapter Four. But when all is said and done, I do want to lift up these five words: "We shall all be changed." It is true that God is going to change us, to make us pure. I like the *Clear Word* paraphrase of this wonderful verse: "In a moment, in the blink of an eye, God will change us. Sinful bodies will be replaced with sinless ones, and beings with a limited life span will receive a life that never ends."

I fully agree with my friend who wrote this letter: we need to be changed before heaven is a fit home for us. As C. S. Lewis wrote in his masterpiece, *The Problem of Pain*, if we're not willing to "eat the only food that the universe grows," the holy diet of heaven, what can we do but starve? But thank God, we have this promise that God will accomplish all heaven's objectives in us. And notice as well: "In a moment, in the twinkling of an eye, at the last trump."

A recent challenging book by the late Andrews University professor Samuele Bacchiocchi, entitled *Resurrection or Immortality?*, is hard going in spots, but right at the end he writes about the utter *reality* of heaven, the incredible realness of life there.

"Whatever the meaning of all the details, the vision of the Holy City conveys the image, not of a mystical, monastic life in a heavenly retreat, but of urban life of intense activity on this renewed earth. . . . Our resurrection bodies will experience the *glory* of an inner and outward transformation."[1]

Some Bible versions, instead of incorruptible, say this: "Imperishable." Because the trumpet is going to sound, and you and I, if we're willing, will be changed into something fit for heaven, something holy, something imperishable. The composer of the *Messiah* died at the age of seventy-four; that incredible gift, that genius, was cut short. Imagine the music an immortal, imperishable George Frederick Handel might be able to give us, WILL be able to give us when the trumpet sounds again.

Worthy is the Lamb that was slain, and hath redeemed us to God by His blood, to receive power, and riches, and wisdom, and strength, and honor, and glory, and blessing. Blessing and honor, glory and power, be unto Him that sitteth upon the throne, and unto the Lamb, for ever and ever. Amen. Revelation 5:12, 13

21

Worthy Is the Lamb

Anywhere you travel in the world, it's always an exciting development when a new man or woman is suddenly thrust into a position of prominence, of power. Before they were just one of the masses . . . oh, maybe a governor or senator or alderman. But all at once–*boom!* They occupy the top spot of authority.

I've probably tormented you enough with musings about the American electoral process, so imagine instead a small child growing up in some far-flung distant corner of the globe. He or she goes to school and mingles with others. There is nothing particularly extraordinary about this anonymous kid; they put on their pants one leg at a time; they play with their Christmas toys and wear out the batteries on their new gadgets. They experience failures and successes–and then, to the astonishment of some and the despair of others, are suddenly the occupants of Number Ten

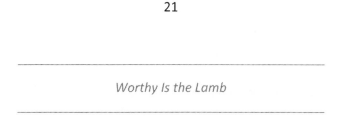

Downing Street. Or the new President of France. Chancellor of Germany. King of Thailand.

And again the citizens ask: should these people receive such power? Are they worthy? Are they deserving? I'm technologically ashamed to admit it, but when I first worked on some of this material for the holiday radio series, I actually looked up some reference material on an Encarta CD-ROM! Can you imagine? But the encyclopedia article about Handel got rather flowery, calling him "one of the greatest composers of the late baroque period and, during his lifetime, perhaps the most internationally famous of *all* musicians . . . [with] rich and unique musical genius." Does he deserve that kind of praise and glory?

Well, there's one time that question is asked, and you don't have to run a poll or watch CNN's World Report or let cable titans Sean Hannity and Rachel Maddow duke it out in order to discover the answer. Because every Christmas we think about a little Baby born to this world. And even as a newborn infant, He was in a position of power. Even in that manger, in a barn, this shriveled, crying, Baby with the cut cord like any other baby . . . was a King. And we hear the choir sing: "Come and worship, Come and worship, Worship Christ, the newborn King."

But the onlooker asks: Why? Worship a little Baby? Why? What has He done to deserve it? Why do these "three kings of Orient" bow down, kneel down, touch their foreheads to the ground for a Baby? England's Theresa May and Donald Trump have at least earned some respect with all those votes cast for them. But why does this unknown Baby, born to two young people not even married, have a right, not only to our respect, but our worship?

We find the answer to that question in the book of Revelation, and also in this great anthem from Handel's *Messiah*. It comes right at the end; in fact, this is the final chorus, #53: *Worthy Is the Lamb* and then the long, majestic *Amen* which runs seven pages. But here is Revelation 5:12, 13:

Worthy is the Lamb that was slain to receive power, and riches, and wisdom, and strength, and honor, and glory, and blessing. And every creature which is in heaven, and on the earth, and under the earth, and such as are in the sea, and all that are in them, heard I saying, Blessing and honor, and glory, and power, be unto Him that sitteth upon the throne, and unto the Lamb for ever and ever.

Well, we get the answer immediately about WHY this Baby deserves the power and the riches and the glory. It's because He's the Lamb. Worthy is the *Lamb* that was slain. It's not because He was born in a manger that He was worthy. It's not because He performed miracles. It's not because the Sermon on the Mount is quotable and an effective blueprint for spiritual harmony. It's not because He healed the sick.

No, it's because He grew to be a Man and because that Man, at the age of thirty-three, went to a hill called Calvary and He paid the price for my sins and for your sins. And *that* is why He is worthy; that is why we say, "Give Him the honor! Give Him the power! We can trust Him with the power because He's the Lamb, because of what He did! Let's give Him the glory because He earned it on a hill far, far, away."

I have haltingly, and with many false starts and feeble steps, come to a personal Christian theology that runs exactly nine words: *Jesus paid it all; all to Him I owe.* He died to give me eternal life; by all that I know of mathematical equations, I must–and I earnestly want to–worship and love and obey Him forever.

Notice that the whole universe joins in on this chorus. Every creature on this earth, to be sure, but also those in heaven and on the far-flung worlds of God's vast universe. "A hundred billion angels," says one paraphrase version. They all watched the Baby get born; they watched Him grow up. And then they watched as He gave Himself as the Lamb. So if you want surround-sound power as it's sung by people in all corners of the universe–north, south, east, west, up, down, near and far–this is the song. "Worthy is the Lamb!"

But now a question for each of you still reading. And this may be our final point of contact, these last few moments. You and I might never again "connect up" again. I may never get the chance to say this again to you.

So here goes: "What about *you*?" Meaning: what will *you* do about this infant Christ child, this Lamb?

Does He receive honor and glory? Yes, but does He receive it from you? "All power be unto Him," some of us sing. And the angels and the saints. But friend, do *you* sing it today? Jesus lives today, and He does have power, but does He have it for your life? Do you give Him that authority?

I like that praise song: "Lord of all, of all seen and unseen things. Of a universe that sings and calls you Lord of all. Lord of all, of the power not to sin. You have always been, and always will be . . . Lord of all." And yet we come to this moment, this one spiritual crossroad, on Christmas Eve or whatever your calendar says right now, where *you* decide if He will be your Lord. Think of that word–LORD–and what it implies for you. Lord of *all*; does that include you?

Marjorie Lewis Lloyd, who penned many classic messages for the *It Is Written* television program, once observed: "If we are on a sinking ship, it is not enough to *applaud* the lifeboat. We must *get into it*."

And she's right. Friend, this Lamb *is* worthy. Why not play Track #53 right now, and in the next three-and-a-half minutes, decide that He's forever worthy of your love?

Amen

AUTHOR'S NOTE: If it is indeed December as you read this, Lisa and I would love to wish you a very Christ-centered Merry Christmas! I hope the message of this book has touched your soul and brought music into the glory of your holiday.

Please feel free to drop by our web page, www.davidbsmith-books.com, and see what else is available for your reading pleasure. I'm especially grateful for the beautiful job the publishers did on *Finding Waldo*, the story of my dad's Hollywood experience in the *Our Gang* movie franchise back in the 1930s. If there are young people in your family, they'll enjoy the ten volumes in the sports-oriented Christian adventure series, *Bucky Stone*. Each book is available in both print and electronic formats, and are priced to be great stocking-stuffers.

Best of all . . . our exciting inspirational series of love stories set in Bangkok is ready for you to enjoy and share as Christmas gifts. I spent a wonderful childhood in Thailand as a missionary kid, and have folded so many memories and Holy Spirit miracles into these adventures. Every story does have a first date, a first kiss, and a nice finish that includes an engagement ring! I hope you get a sweet blessing and the stirring of happy memories as you read.

Bibliography

Chapter One

1. Roger A. Bullard, *Messiah,* (Grand Rapids, William B. Eerdsman Publishing Company, 1993), 12
2. *Adventist Bible Commentary, Vol. 4* (Washington, D.C., Review and Herald Publishing Association, 1955), 245

Chapter Two

1. Bullard, 13

Chapter Four

1. C. S. Lewis, *Surprised By Joy,* contained in *The Inspired Writings of C. S. Lewis* (New York, Inspirational Press, 1994), 125
2. C. S. Lewis, *Letters to Malcolm* (San Diego, Harcourt, 1964), 108, 109
3. C. S. Lewis, *Mere Christianity,* (New York, Collier Books, 1943), 181, 182

Chapter Five

1. Jan Karon, *The Mitford Bedside Companion,* (New York, Viking, 2006), 401
2. John Shelby Spong, *Why Christianity Must Change or Die*, (San Francisco, Harper, 1998), 12
3. Philip Yancey, *The Jesus I Never Knew* (Grand Rapids, Zondervan Publishing House, 1995), 30

Chapter Six

1. Philip Yancey, *The Jesus I Never Knew*, 159
2. Ibid, *Disappointment With God* (New York, Harper Collins, 1988) 138
3. Ibid, *The Jesus I Never Knew*, 160
4. Ibid, *Disappointment With God*, 140

Chapter Eight

1. Yancey, *The Jesus I Never Knew*, 36

Chapter Nine

1. Adrian Rogers, *Expect a Miracle But Believe in Jesus*, (Wheaton, IL, Crossway Books, 1997), 19-22

Chapter Ten

1. E. G. White, *The Desire of Ages,* (Mountain View, CA, Pacific Press Publishing Association, 1898), 512

Chapter Twelve

1. Bullard, 74

Chapter Fifteen

1. Billy Graham, *Just As I Am* (San Francisco, HarperCollins, 1997), 693

Chapter Sixteen

1. Tom Brokaw, *The Finest Generation,* (New York, Dell Publishing, 1998), 156, 157
2. Ibid, 353-355
3. *Adventist Bible Commentary, Vol. 3,* 687, 688

Chapter Twenty

1. Samuele Bacchiocchi, *Immortality or Resurrection,* (Berrien Springs, MI, Biblical Perspectives, 1997)*, 290*